Worship Musician/

Presents

THE WORSHIP BAND BOOK

THE WORSHIP BAND BOOK

Training and Empowering Your Worship Band

Tom Lane

ROWMAN & LITTLEFIELD
Lanham • Boulder • New York • London

Published in 2012 by Rowman & Littlefield
An Imprint of The Rowman & Littlefield Publishing Group
4501 Forbes Boulevard, Suite 200
Lanham, Maryland 20706

Book design by Mayapriya Long, Bookwrights

Library of Congress Cataloging-in-Publication Data
Lane, Tom, 1965-
  The worship band book : training and empowering your worship band / Tom Lane.
       pages cm
  Includes index.
  1. Church music–Handbooks, manuals, etc. 2. Contemporary Christian music–Vocational guidance. I. Title.
  ML3001.L36 2012
  264'.2–dc23
                        2012007929

ISBN 978-1-4584-1817-3

To my parents, Tommy and Margie Lane,
who committed me to the Lord as a child, encouraged me endlessly,
and gave me both opportunity and freedom to pursue my passion!

Contents

Foreword

There are many different types of worship-leading musicians around these days—and of course, some extreme examples along the way. Some people might have a great deal of heart and yet not think too much about the art of how they create and lead. There could be some real and raw devotion in the mix, but they never really get to grips with how to communicate it in an inspiring and skillful way. At the other extreme, we find worship musicians who've spent so many hours learning musical chops, and yet somehow, for all of the accomplished musicianship, they're strangely lacking in passion. I guess we all find ourselves somewhere along this spectrum, but the point is this: the very best worship leaders join these two strands together in beautiful harmony. Their leading is the explosive overflow of the heart, and yet it's guided by a strong sense of creative skill and purpose. Psalm 78 tells us that King David led the people with "skillful hands and integrity of heart," and that should be our aim also.

The first time I ever met Tom Lane, he was playing electric guitar with a refreshing brilliance and musicality. I soon realized he wasn't even using any guitar effects in that moment, and yet the tone was incredible. I therefore concluded God must have given him "magic guitar-fingers" or something equally spiritual! The sounds coming out of that instrument and the sensitivity with which he was playing were simply amazing. And yet of course, the secret lay elsewhere. For his touch and tone on that electric guitar were the result of years and years practice. That might have been impressive enough in and of itself. But I have also seen Tom away from the spotlight, loving God and leading people through His thoughts, words, and deeds. I have seen him mentoring other musicians and speaking powerfully and consistently into their lives. It's the very same mixture we saw exampled above in the life of King David—the dynamic combination of heart and art.

This book will give an opportunity for you to be mentored by Tom too. I'm confident that his practical approach and spiritual wisdom will give you much insight and inspiration for the journey.

Play well and bow low, for the glory of God!

—Matt Redman

Preface

Worship hasn't long been considered an industry and genre of music. Growing up I attended the "worship service" every week, where we sang hymns and sing-a-long choruses and listened to the preacher preach. I equated worship only with an event that I had to attend because my father served the church as a minister of music. The early Jesus music was making its way into the Church through youth groups. Not until the mid '80s to early '90s did you hear terms like worship leaders, praise teams, and praise bands.

The Contemporary Christian Music industry was catapulted into existence by the Jesus movement, led by hippies and surfers. Though it grew into a profitable and thriving industry, it started with raw passion and hunger. A young generation growing tired of the old. Sound familiar? It's a pattern throughout Church history and humanity in general. The CCM industry weakened as modern worship songs, and the artists and leaders at the helm of this new movement, began to eclipse CCM. A few heralds and forerunners began moving away from the herd, so to speak, and seeking God's presence and voice again. What arose were heart cries and ground swells around the globe. Though we can attach names and faces to some of them, it was God doing the stirring. Record labels then scurried to create worship music and find worship artists, whereas *worship* wasn't really on the radar shortly before in that sense. Many in the Church still considered worship to be fanatical and hyperemotional. The earliest praise and worship music was predominately coming out of charismatic Churches and not tolerated by many of the more conservative groups. So worship has evolved, and journeyed a long way in just the past 20 years alone.

Just over a decade ago, one song brought an important issue front and center for the Church. To me it was the banner call for our generation, *to return to our first love as God's people*. Matt Redman's "Heart of Worship": "A song in itself is not what You have required/I'm coming back to the heart of worship and it's all about You/All about You Jesus." Ultimately it's not about artists, worship leaders, career opportunities, commerce, or Church programming. Though the Church supports iconic names and ministries that have shaped Church and culture, it's still about The Lord. The struggle is to keep that the main thing. Any time we deviate from this aim, God will lovingly, mercifully, and sometimes forcefully remind us.

Worship took on a whole new meaning for me personally when I came to grips with God and the shallow, puny little box I had allowed Him to exist in. I didn't start liking worship songs till my own heart began to change and desire to engage with God during worship times, versus being a spectator of the program. It came through brokenness, pain, and hunger for more of the God I read about in my Bible, not just the God I knew growing up in a conservative Church.

My journey has led me through 30 years in music and ministry, many experiences, and great relationships in both the Church and music industry. I have a deep love and appreciation for the Church and her diversity. I'm not as keen as I once was to espouse my own opinions; rather, I want to see the Church healthy and holy, in order to reflect God as He really is, not as a distorted religious image wrought of human traditions.

My heart is huge for creative people, but also for leaders in Churches of all shapes and sizes. The collection of articles in this book—each written at a different time, and many in different places around the world—are intended to be a shot in the arm, to prod us further along a road laden with messy though well-intentioned people. That's the Church! We're messy, selfish, ambitious, but loved dearly by God. We are the very bunch through whom He has chosen to reveal His love and image to the world. What we call the worship time is really a way of life, meant to reflect His mercy, compassion, and righteousness to all. To do that, we need to encourage one another up, not tear one another down. We're not in competition but relationship.

Holiness begins with humble, broken, and repentant lives. *Holy* means "whole," and we can't be that if we really believe we don't need inner change, which only comes to penitent people. Good worship is not as much about good music as it is good time spent in the presence of God. Not to take one thing away from the good that's come from skill, technology, and passion, but now more than ever, the Church needs to continue to make room for God to move, live, and breathe in our corporate gatherings.

I've attempted to shoot as straight as I can and cover as many bases as possible. All to help creative people and ministry leaders, join their efforts, and be unified. To become a powerful expression of Christ's Body. I don't know it all, and I don't know anyone that does. The expressions of worship change from place to place, because we are a body compiled of many parts, not just one. What I do here is not always what you need to do there to be the most effective. Who we need is God, and what we need is a real visitation from Him day in and day out, Monday through Sunday.

My prayer is that you enjoy and put to use some of the things that I've suggested, take the good and forget the rest. The challenge is to be more honest, real, excellent, teachable, and creative for His glory above our own. My experience is that we know a lot about creativity and not enough about the call. I hope to bring balance, as I believe we are only as effective as we are truly surrendered to God's best plans, not just cool programs.

Whether rock band, worship band, worship team, musician, singer, or artist, we can be used to minister to The Lord, His people, and the world, but it starts in the heart!

Acknowledgments

Patty, My Love, thank you for loving God the way you do, sharing life and love with me, and giving so much to others. I still marvel at our second chance—our miracle marriage and the incredible wife you are to me.

Pop and Mama Lane, thank you for your sacrifice, support, and guidance throughout my life that enabled me to do what I do. You are wonderful parents—and Pop, you're a true Maestro!

BJ and Rubia Hoagland, thank you for giving your daughter to me! Your light shines bright through her life every day.

Worship Musician! magazine and Bruce Adolph, thanks for including me! Matt Kees, you just plain rock!

A special thanks to the following companies, which I proudly endorse, and which not only have helped me greatly through the years but serve the Church in more ways than most know! Avalon Guitars; Doug Gould at Worship MD; D'addario; Planet Waves; John Chandler at Pedal Train/Pro Stage Gear; the guys at Yamaha Commercial Audio and Musical Instruments: Mike Overlin, Dan Craik, Jacob Cody, Mark Rush; Shure; JHS Pedals.

Definitions in the text are from the Apple Dictionary.

1

Band on a Mission

The mission of a worship band is to highlight and focus people on the Father, Son, and Holy Spirit and God's beautiful attributes. I like to say that it's bringing God to the center of a room and creating an atmosphere for people to speak directly to Him. Out of this centering flows some monumental things. It washes people with the much-needed truth, heals a broken heart, and takes our eyes off ourselves to see the broken world around us. Exalting and adoring God with our affections and confessions draws His presence, and in God's presence, life takes place for a community of followers, and outsiders see that there is life beyond what they've known. Although creativity and coolness are appreciated, and reaction is fun, the band that takes their eyes off the goal of God as center will simply be creative and cool and getting external reactions.

—Charlie Hall, Singer-Songwriter, Leader

The Mission

Years ago I was at a festival in southern Hungary with people from all over the world. We were there to help encourage artists and musicians. Bands came from Greece, Serbia, Romania, Poland, Hungary, Turkey, and Macedonia. The Turkish band was one of the only known Christian bands in their country and paid a dear price to even be Christian. As I talked with these bands, it was evident they had a mission and were passionate for Christ despite opposition, inconvenience, and lack of resources. Just to get to the event, some of them passed through war zones in Bosnia, Croatia, and Serbia.

We are fortunate in our country to have the possibility of choosing music as a profession or being involved with worship and ministry vocationally. We live in a world of big events, tour busses, and stars. I'm amazed by the passion and drive creative people have innately, but when joined with a passion for what pleases the God who made them—it's even more amazing. Since most of the bands at the festival didn't have an option to do music for a living, they were focused on serving the needs around them and going where many wouldn't dare go to play. As I heard their stories, I was continuously humbled and convicted. The professionals from Nashville had come to help them, but truly they had more right than many of the so-called professionals. Christian music for them wasn't the possibility of notoriety or platform, because it didn't exist. Not to take away anything from those genuinely used by God on a world stage, but the "stuff" can be distracting.

Let's live with a strong sense of mission. It's easy to use words like *ministry* and *worship* to our advantage when what we may want is exposure. We can all be egocentric and selfish! King David was rich and famous, so that's not the issue either. Being about the mission of Jesus is! Since God is famous for promoting whom He chooses, what, if any, amount of our time should be spent promoting ourselves? I don't presume to know what you specifically are called to do or how best to do it, only to remind you of Matthew 6:33: "Seek the Kingdom of God first!" Be humble and He will exalt you.

Humanity craves its heroes and icons. For many the prospect of fame is alluring. It's also tempting for us to judge or criticize them from afar, but that's not our job. We've all seen the rise and fall of many good people with great talent who are just as real and vulnerable as the rest. Paul reminded us that we're in a battle against a real adversary. For that reason, we strive to avoid pitfalls that can waylay anyone. As we write our vision/mission statements and take our art to the masses, remember that we are first created for His pleasure and He'll have no other god before Him.

Is your goal the pursuit of God and His pleasure? Worship is that above all, not living only to accomplish our dreams or even to please the Church. Jesus preached the gospel and lived a life of mercy. He spent less time tailoring what He said and did specifically for the religious community and more time aiming at the hearts of sick people. We can all be guilty of ignoring the religion that God accepts as pure and faultless in James 1:27, but let's don't be in this generation! It's never ultimately about us or the music. Worship and justice go together always.

When I met the very hardcore Serbian band, I was astonished to find they were young evangelists and pastors that understood the mission clearly and so chose to be servants first. My thought was: these guys are truly modeling what it means to be Christian, and they're a band.

Bands come and go. What are you doing that's lasting? What are you doing without a record deal or money behind you that's worthy of supporting? Be more than creative geniuses, and do now what you're called to do; don't wait for discovery to start! The awesome thing is that God loves to give you the desires of your heart and will honor pure lives that pray for His will to be done. The secret is to be on *The Mission* as in Matthew 28:18, not just a mission!

Why Do You Do What You Do?

It's a great question, and we should have an answer for it. Anything can become routine; more than one have reached cruising altitude, leveled off, and switched to autopilot. Once something works, it's hard to change or even see the need to. It's sad to see once fruitful ministries lose their effectiveness, continuing on the old track to the point where some take advantage of the ones that have supported them. If nothing else, we should be faithful to please and honor God with what we do.

So why do we do what we do? If you're a band or leader, I encourage you not to be aloof or vague in your mission. If your desire is to be a star or have your music or songs circle the globe and reach the CCLI Top 100 list, then that's not the utmost for His highest. Though artists live to create and have others take notice of our work, we should please God first. If He chooses to promote, then it's His doing.

As I travel and worship in differing streams of the Church, I see that God is calling out this next generation of musicians and artists, *who are worshippers*, to go to different places and levels than many Churches are prepared to let them go and are comfortable with. I also see a host of creative talents with not much idea of what God's really calling them to do. The most common thing I hear is: God is calling me to sing. But singing isn't a calling! It's a talent that we steward. Many seem to confuse desire and talents with calling.

We do what we do in order to fulfill the call of God on our lives and seek His kingdom. If you are in a band and really want to hit the target you were designed for, then do all you can to understand what that target is according to God's word. It's not enough to just want to go out and sing or play. In addition to being talented, you have gifts that are there to build up and serve.

There are some wonderful movements worldwide producing great new music, most of which are building on strong values and relationships. Their aim is not first to promulgate artists, *in the name of worship leaders,* to the forefront of Christendom. Ironically, as they focus on the basics of a Jesus lifestyle and serving others, the music seems to arise naturally and traverse the world. That's a Godly model, I think.

Do what you are really here to do, and let God pour out His blessing on it! We need bands and leaders that create and play for God's pleasure, not solely their own—who will lead a lost world to the knowledge and truth of Jesus. Whether your songs are congregational or not, you can be used of God. But He won't pour out blessing beyond what you are ready to steward well. Living a lifestyle of holiness makes you ready; good music alone won't. I love to see bands with raw energy and creativity, balanced by maturity and humility. That comes only by laying your creative vision down and taking up the mission of Jesus. If you do that first, no doubt you may find yourself with unique opportunities.

At the end of the day, no single musician or leader can boil the band-worship ministry down to a formula nor should attempt to. God is bigger, wiser—full of creativity and life—and has chosen to let it flow through messed-up people. So it's not about us anyway. As a band, go for it, but live it! Don't just sing about it or use acceptable Christian lingo to sell your songs or records. Be honest and be pure. Serve God by loving those in your own world. Take Jesus to your streets and communities. Be artistic and excellent, but *be* the Church!

Finally, know why you do what you do. "Seek first the kingdom of God and His righteousness and all these things will be added unto you" (Matt. 6:33).

Practice and Play God's Way

One night while in Switzerland working, I was unable to sleep, so I flipped on the TV. There were only a few channels to choose from, and I found two programs. The first was a tribute to George Harrison, who had died that day; I was finding this out for the first time. The other was a Deep Purple concert with Steve Morse playing guitar. I'm showing my age here, but both were my musical heroes, so I flipped back and forth between the programs till they were over.

I was sad to learn the news of George and struck by how they emphasized his spirituality. He was unashamed of what he believed. No matter what you believe, it is contagious and inspiring when you're unashamedly passionate about it. I don't ultimately know where his heart was, but he seemed to play and live with conviction.

We focus a lot on the "how-to's" of worship and being skillful. There are some great resources to help us become better, yet apart from God's spirit, what we do, say, or sing is empty. We lead others nowhere, even hinder them, when we forget or neglect to please God first with our lives. God's grace is big and covers us even when we mess it all up, but grace shouldn't become an excuse not to strive after holiness.

With all the emphasis that we put on facilitating others in worship, I wanted to remind us that our first call is to minister to The Lord—who has a lot to say about worship, what it is and what it's not. It's not enough to play, sing, and be talented; we can be good, even spiritual, and still miss it. Holiness is the call, not the music.

Romans 12 is a great guide for some practical maintenance of the heart. Take it as you would a prescription to keep yourself well and healthy; it'll make you better.

Romans 12: 1–21:

1. "Offer your bodies as living sacrifices, holy and pleasing to God—this is your spiritual act of worship."

2. "Do not conform any longer to the pattern of this world, but be transformed by the renewing of your mind. Then you will be able to test and approve what God's will is—his good, pleasing, and perfect will."

3. "I say to every one of you: do not think of yourself more highly than you ought, but rather think of yourself with sober judgment, in accordance with the measure of faith God has given you."

4–5. "Just as each of us has one body with many members, and these members do not all have the same function, so in Christ we who are many form one body, and each member belongs to all the others."

6–8. "We have different gifts, according to the grace given us. If a man's gift is prophesying, let him use it in proportion to his faith. If it is serving, let him serve; if it is teaching, let him teach; if it is encouraging, let him encourage; if it is contributing to the needs of others, let him give generously; if it is leadership, let him govern diligently; if it is showing mercy, let him do it cheerfully."

9–13. "Love must be sincere. Hate what is evil; cling to what is good. Be devoted to one another in brotherly love. Honor one another above yourselves.

Never be lacking in zeal, but keep your spiritual fervor, serving The Lord. Be joyful in hope, patient in affliction, faithful in prayer. Share with God's people who are in need. Practice hospitality."

14–16.   "Bless those who persecute you; bless and do not curse. Rejoice with those who rejoice; mourn with those who mourn. Live in harmony with one another. Do not be proud, but be willing to associate with people of low position. Do not be conceited."

17–20.   "Do not repay anyone evil for evil. Be careful to do what is right in the eyes of everybody. If it is possible, as far as it depends on you, live at peace with everyone. Do not take revenge, my friends, but leave room for God's wrath, for it is written: 'It is mine to avenge; I will repay,' says The Lord. On the contrary: 'If your enemy is hungry, feed him; if he is thirsty, give him something to drink. In doing this, you will heap burning coals on his head.'"

21.   "Do not be overcome by evil, but overcome evil with good."

Does it seem strange to use scripture as a way to become a better band? You won't find many trade mags listing it as a Top 10 prescription for success, but if we are Christians involved with worship, let us practice and play God's way!

Choose Well

Recently I stood at "The Crossroads" in the Mississippi Delta, where bluesman Robert Johnson supposedly "made a deal with the devil." Amazingly, the drive and passion of artistry really does lure many away from God's best. As eager as we are to find our dreams, there's a real opponent who'd love to help us aim for the wrong ones and derail us. Choice is a gift and responsibility, and we each can decide whether or not to seek God's Kingdom above our own dreams.

Bands are normally built around someone's creative talent or driving vision. It's easy to rally around and focus on talent, so we have to choose to keep the main thing the main thing. If vision overrides God-given responsibilities and priorities, then we compromise and make deals that ultimately cost us something somewhere down the line. That's the sad story of many bands, starting out friends with enough zeal to save the world and ending up enemies with a world of issues. Most don't last long. Period! My two-cent theory is: We put dreams ahead of relationships and build the wrong things, convinced it's God. We conveniently go back on our word and alter the original vision. Loyalty and relationship seem to mean a lot when we have what we want, but how easily forgotten and overlooked when it all changes. The same is true with band members: like-minded as can be till we have to consider the other opinions in the mix, then we're easily divided. If God's behind our vision one day and not the next, how flaky is that? He's not flaky, so it must be us. If we achieve our dreams without reflecting God's heart and character, then what have we accomplished?

It's my hope that as musicians, we aspire to live by God's wisdom and be the real deal—to be mature, as Paul put it. It's a wonderful thing that God uses any of us as messed up as we are, but let's not use that as an excuse to be goofy and selfish artists while the world looks on. *Your life is your ministry*; the band is an opportunity to let your light shine for His glory. Play great music, but do as Jesus did.

So how important is a band really? Is it worth everything that really matters in your life? Worth sacrificing God's best? I think we'd all say no, but those in one know the pull to gamble it all for the pursuit—even in the name of ministry. Every day we stand at a very real crossroad; we can go our own way or God's way. Choose well!

Here are some safeguards:

1. Don't confuse your dream with what's ultimately important to God: the little things.

2. Fulfill your ministry to God and family first, and protect them with clear boundaries.

3. Don't let the band keep you from being a faithful spouse and friend. Or rob you of healthy relationships.

4. Don't let someone's creative vision or exciting opportunities lure you into unhealthy situations or away from God's best for you.

5. Confront problems and issues head on, and communicate with grace and tact.

6. Serve gladly, but let no ministry dominate or dictate your life.

7. Choose every day to honor and worship God, so that He can establish and promote you.

8. Don't neglect your personal business and responsibility; it's your job, not the band's!

9. Let your yes be yes and your no be no. Deal honestly in everything, and keep confidences to yourself.

10.   Value your bandmates' opinions, treat them as friends, and respect their responsibilities to steward their own lives, as unto God.

Legacy

"If you build it, they will come," a great line from the movie *Field of Dreams*. I remember standing with some buddies in a building in downtown Nashville that hadn't been used in 20 years. It had no windows in it, needed total renovation, and was in a high-crime area. We were young, zealous, passionate, and near-homeless musicians, who'd been arrested by these words in James 1:27: "Pure and undefiled religion is this—to feed the hungry, cloth the poor, visit the widow and orphans in their distress." We'd also been captivated by the story of Nehemiah, who saw his city in ruins and decided to start rebuilding it.

This building was to house a ministry to the poor, born out of our Thursday-night prayer group that had been meeting for years. So our hearts pounded as we prayed over buying it. We were excited, despite the huge task that lay ahead to renovate it. Clear as day, we felt The Lord say, "Build it, and I will bring those who need to come." Naturally the first thing we did, before even sweeping out 20 years' of dust, was build a stage to play on. We didn't even really know what we would do in the building, just that we had to do it.

For the next three years, we opened the doors every Friday night, served coffee, set up our gear, and worshipped. Worship went on for hours, often into the morning— though we didn't plan that. There was no set list, no power point, and half the time we were writing songs on the spot, singing to The Lord from our own hearts. Ultimately, thousands would end up coming through the years for the worship time more than the guest artists.

It was wild for a band of misfit guys, with no name and no plan to be a band, to find ourselves flowing together in worship and leading a ministry. We were four worship leaders leading together, deferring to whomever stepped out and the rest following. It was truly one of the most amazing things I've ever witnessed or been part of.

What grew out of that building was a ministry that fed hundreds of homeless regularly and was a catalyst for freedom for many. We went out to the roughest neighborhoods, set up stages, and played our music. We took the gospel that had changed our lives to the streets of our city. It was very alive, and people from many different Churches came to help us serve. We witnessed policemen, prostitutes, executives, ministers—Church of Christ, Baptists, and Catholics alike—encounter God through worship and serving.

Certainly we were not the most talented bunch around and had our issues. In time we'd fizzle out, due to our own immaturity and mistakes—but God used us. He blessed our loaves and fishes and turned it into a movement—*for a minute anyway.* Meanwhile, He was stirring others just like us around the world, some of whom became household names in Christendom and much more famous than we ever did.

Our story is one to learn from, and that's the reason I'm telling it now. We had loads of zeal but not too much knowledge. Granted we were in our twenties then, but there is much to be said about the character required to hold what God desires to release through His people. The vision was big, and there was passion galore. We were united, and experienced God doing great things through us. I don't negate any of what He did, nor would I trade the struggles for what they've produced in all of our lives. I'm a firm believer that you can do whatever it is that God moves you to do. I'll even be the first to say, Go do it! But I would add a few things to that charge, to help avoid some of our failures.

1. God is always most interested in our maturity and character, because it produces the fruit in our lives. Many a misguided musician/band have set out to do great things for God but fallen short. Usually because it becomes more about a name or success. Success is when we're dead enough that He shines through us. God will always test your wine skin to see if it's fit to hold new wine.

2. Waiting on God's timing is easier to say than do, no doubt. We received numerous words about what God was doing with us and had visions of the masses coming to Christ through us. But we were derailed by our own weaknesses and relationship struggles in the flurry of activity. Fast growth is exciting and will have you convinced that God is all in it, but be careful not to let the work become more important than waiting on Him and loving people well. He's not afraid to pass the torch on to another.

3. Listen to the Godly counsel around you; plans succeed with many counselors. We may think we know how to do it on our own, but we don't. There's a really fine line between going for it and walking it out with wisdom. Community helps us remain grounded, sane, and healthy when successes come in life.

4. Finally, when God does give the green light, go with all your might, but do so in humility and hold it all lightly. Paul learned to be content with a little or a lot; we too need to rest in the current moment, *now.* David, just

after being anointed the new king, went right back to shepherding, because that's who he was. Let God exalt you in the right time, and when He does, it will be more than you could ever do on your own.

There's a lot God can do through creative people who dare to dream and build something. Build a legacy of holiness! Be the best band you can be, but be who and what God wants you to be first.

Relevant Lives

Musicians and artists provide a backdrop for living and help shape the Church and culture. With this influence, we have an even greater responsibility to steward the talents we're given by God, for a purpose. Where we may miss it is in not understanding who we are and what we're called to in the first place. Instead of leading the way, we're often following the paths of others' proven successes. And what band, artist, or musician doesn't want success or affirmation? But we are indeed supposed to be leading.

To know where we need to go, we must know from where we come. If we believe what we say we do about the hope and glory of our God through faith in Christ, then we have to first accept and acknowledge that the call is to Him and His will. In the days of chivalry, knights rode out and fought in the name of their king. They carried his permission, authority, power, and backing. Our king, *the King of Kings*, has clearly commissioned us to carry this hope-filled, good-news gospel to the dying world we live in. Love has to be the underlying motivation. We are living, breathing, modern-day priests, servants, and examples—endowed with the Spirit of Almighty God. We're not simply looking to replicate movements of the past or camp out on history, we are moving toward an end. Our King will return and again has forewarned us to watch, wait, and be prepared for His coming.

"Therefore every teacher of the law who has been instructed about the kingdom of heaven is like the owner of a house who brings out of his storeroom new treasures as well as old" (Matt. 13:52).

As creatively gifted Christians, we have a mandate to live, a story to tell, a role to play, a responsibility to steward, and a future to look forward to and prepare for. Our context is the community of believers that we are a part of, each serving a distinctively different purpose, according to the gifts and talents we have. Drawing out treasures from the storeroom of faith and not an empty well. The mandate is not to hole up away from the world in seclusion as creative hermits. We are to be very much involved and present within it, *just not of it.* We don't worship its way or do life its way. We don't copy, we create. Resident within us is the beauty of the One True God who made the Earth and stars, and the same power that raised Him from the grave. We do have a new song to sing.

We also have a choice: to aim for targets that are of human design or to fulfill a divine destiny that we were made for. For many talented people, this is a huge challenge, as their dreams are in contrast to what they're called to do and often win out over God's "plan A." There's absolutely nothing wrong with our works and expressions being promulgated to places of renown or importance. What matters is *who* does the promoting. Chasing success at any cost will surely cost more than we ever imagined. History proves that God can make us famous in an instant if He decides to, also that He can take it all away as fast is it comes. We want to be about His business, faithful in the little, which is the fastest track to being ready for success His way.

The first question we have to answer rightly is, "Whose glory are we doing it for?" Laying down our burdens and dreams at the Cross of Jesus is daunting, because it usually requires having our fingers pried off of things dearest to our hearts. I've always loved the analogy of a wild horse being bridled; once tamed and harnessed, all of its innate strength and power is subject to the control and direction of the skilled rider. In our case, God is the most merciful master we could ever hope to be fully surrendered to. Once harnessed, our talents, gifts, and entire being are now in the hands of the Supreme Archer. He can, and will, fire at will all of the arrows in the quiver *that are ready to be fired.*

Where do you want to be? What do you want to do? There's freedom yet immense responsibility with The Lord. We can ask what we will, but we must ask in His name. We can go wherever, but He directs the steps ultimately. We can do anything, but not all things are profitable and worthy in His eyes. The other side of free will is consequence! We will reap what we sow, and it comes down to choosing Christ first in all things. No one can make us read and understand the road map we've been given in His word. But if we do seek the Wisdom of God that it contains, He will miraculously open our spiritual eyes and give understanding. Because He gives gifts and doesn't take them back. But He will also allow us to go our own way, and many do.

We live in a time when there are more resources than ever available to us in order to improve the quality and excellence in worship. But technology and skill are not adequate substitutes for the posture of our hearts. As good as we may sound or prepared as we may be, the point of our worship is to honor The Lord with our lives—then our music and art will have a greater impact on the world we live in. If all we do doesn't point and lead people to the cross of Christ, then it's in vain.

Let's guard our hearts and minds from being lured away by our own ambitions, and lead the way by serving God first with our worship.

Band of Brothers

Jonathan is a good example of the right response to God choosing someone else. Although it would have been normal to be threatened by the prophecy naming David Israel's next king instead of himself, the true blood heir of Saul, Jonathan, committed himself to doing everything he could to make David successful. He rejoiced in telling his friend, "You will be king over Israel and I will be next to you" (1 Samuel 23:17). Those who humble themselves under God's almighty hand will be exalted in due time (1 Peter 5:6). As the story unfolds, Jonathan and David become a true band of brothers—devoted allies for the greatest good of God's glory.

One of the hardest things for creative people to surrender is glory and credit. Though we sing "It's all about You, Jesus," if we're honest, there's a small part that wants it to be at least a little about us. I have sung and played on a few projects where they forgot to put my name in the liner credits. On one in particular, we were told after working for hours that they'd not be listing any of the musicians or singers, so as to avoid paying scale wages and residuals for our work. I admit it bothered me a lot! Ultimately I had to get over it and realize that it doesn't matter in eternity anyway. It's a test we'll likely face in our journey at some point.

If you look at successful partnerships in music, there's usually a face or name that everybody recognizes and a sidekick that has more than likely contributed equally—but is the lesser known. I've always admired the ones who have quietly accepted their roles and are content just to share in the success, though faceless and nameless. There's a saying I've heard and reflected on my whole life; it goes roughly like this: "Carry another man across the bridge and you will have arrived there yourself." What a way to live!

What is the goal of a worship band? If we know that leading worship is not about the worship leader, why do we envy or compete for the position? If God is looking at the heart first, why do we critique and judge others' performances? If we believe that unity brings the blessing of God, then the goal is honoring our King. If we truly desire to do that, why would we ever argue and fight over the stuff we do in Churches and worship teams? Much of the small stuff causes us to miss the point. We may never really enter into worship at all if we're more spectator than participant! We can also forfeit experiencing the real power of God's presence if we are so easily swayed and distracted from the goal.

As you come to the worship platform to serve, I encourage you to aim for taking the high road, resist the urge to criticize, focus your own heart, and prefer others even when it hurts. Unfortunately, the Church can be one of the most critical places to serve. Usually people criticize because we believe down deep that we can do it better or deserve the opportunity over another. We can only control what we do. There'll always be others chosen over or before us, and inevitably someone will receive, maybe even accept, praise that is duly ours, but what we do with that is what counts. What if we all aimed to be nameless and faceless—and learned to be okay with it? To be used in any way to make Jesus more famous is the ultimate honor and privilege. That's what we should become good at and known for.

What we treasure and love most is what we chase after. It is a real temptation, and always has been, to envy and aspire to another's high position. As you look around you in the worship world that is now a genre and an industry presenting real opportunities, I only want to remind you to keep your focus on the pursuit of Christ. If we are to genuinely encounter God working in and among us, then we must pursue Him first and above all in worship. More than sounding and looking good, we need worship leaders, bands, and artists— chasing after His heart and purpose, not simply the business and performance of music.

Turns out Jonathan and David each needed the other desperately to do what they were created to do. Likewise, we need each other as we learn to play our own roles, without grumbling or disputing—contently!

Retooled

retool. To reorganize something in order to make it more efficient or powerful.

The landscape of the music industry has been changing for some time. Voilà, we're in a new and very different day that's causing many to reinvent themselves in order to contend and survive. It's not an easy thing to do any time you're settled into a groove or rut.

The following was said of New York Giants coach Tom Coughlin, just after leading the underdog wild-card team to world championship in Super Bowl 43: "He's reinvented his veneer and reconnected with his team." Adapting is part of change, and in the coach's case, some of it apparently came in response to others recognizing his need to change in some specific areas. Guess he embraced and applied it, with some good results. Unless you're a Patriots fan; then, *sorry!*

Since I'm not qualified to judge, I won't start pointing out everyone else's specifics, but I will admit my own. I was always a song leader and learned to do it well as a kid. The real change in my life as a worship leader came when I starting yearning and learning to pour out my heart and prayers to God in songs—without thought or fear of anyone else's understanding, approval, or criticism. I truly found freedom, and it makes it hard to go backwards. Here's my little confession: today, as much as I genuinely love to worship, I am extremely tired of and exhausted by leading worship in a "not so modern" context. The music is a bit more exciting, but *sometimes* it feels just as formulaic and programmed now as Church did to me twenty-five years ago—with very little freedom.

So I admit it, I struggle with the structure-and-form issue, but that gives me no right to develop a critical or cynical attitude towards Churches that do it the same way, week in and week out. Nor does it make me any more special that I have found some freedom—which I get to live out anyway, since worship isn't about the hour-a-week meeting for me. What it challenges me to ask is: "What change do I need to make in order to continue serving His Church with a pure and right heart?" It's not important or productive to impose my own agenda or freedom on others' context. The goal is God being lifted up, then drawing us unto Himself. He can work in 15 minutes or 3 hours, it's up to Him. Normally the struggle is more about getting out of our own way and/or His, enough to be used and experience His presence.

I am constantly plowing through whatever my perceived or imposed limitations are in a given situation, to begin my own engagement with God. It starts with humbling myself, thanking Him, and confessing to Him. Once I've done that long enough, I usually forget all about obstacles and feel no need to manipulate or control worship at all—just to serve in the current place, with the best heart I can. If you could be a fly on the wall of my brain and hear the inner dialogue I sometimes go through to get there, it's quite comical but very real, as yours is to you.

More than being subjects of the shifting tide within the music industry, we are, I think, living a change of seasons. God is always moving and at work to accomplish His plans. Change really shouldn't surprise us at all, but it does, and it's uncomfortable. That's because there's more He wants to do in the world. And guess who He's chosen to do it through? The Church!

Regardless of the mission as a band or artist, we first have a responsibility to stand up, be counted as worshippers, and lead the world to Jesus—as opposed to looking to them to tell us how to do it. There's nothing to fear from industry changes or market shifts, unless of course they drive us. Let's seek God for the changes He'd have us make and face them head on.

Change should inspire—and lead us to assess—the need for reinvention and transformation into His likeness. It should also lovingly force us to reconnect with our team, The Body of Christ. The benefits are: It keeps us safe within community and in right relationships. We sharpen one another on the journey to wholeness and maturity in Christ. It's part of God's holy way, and there's no way around it—I've tried it.

My pastor is a longtime friend and a fellow musician who spent many years on the road in ministry. He says, "Being a pastor is the last thing I ever saw myself doing," but the season changed for him and his wife years ago, and they naturally found themselves serving in a different capacity. It didn't come without aches and pains and has required them to make changes for sure, but it's exactly where he needs to be—and the most fulfilling thing he does now, whereas music used to be. We need not fear the change; God intends it for our good!

Here's a wee bit of uncomfortable truth: not all who have a talent need to mortgage the farm to go pursue a career with it. And not all who want to serve need to be on the worship team. Somebody just said "amen" and mentioned a tambourine player by name, didn't you? Admit it! If we're in a rut, I believe the rut is a mindset of entitlement in the Church. Just because we think or feel something doesn't mean it's supposed to be done our way. We don't have a right to it. Talent is what we steward, and gifts are what we use to edify The Body of Christ. We function best when we are completely surrendered—willing to do whatever God asks of us. And often, it's not the way we picture it.

We can serve The Body by playing or singing, but we first lay down our lives at the cross, and He gives them back retooled for the purpose He intended—however different from ours. That's especially applicable and relevant to relationships. Just try exerting unconditional love, patience, support, and encouragement all the time, in every situation, when it really counts and where it really hurts. Normally we draw the line somewhere, usually when people get into our space and want to alter it with their messiness. Imagine that!

At some point, God may send some real, live human to our doorstep, to lovingly poke the finger right in our chest and suggest we grow up! When He does, let it build you up—not tear you down—and cause you to examine your veneer in comparison to the light and life of Jesus, then change accordingly.

If God is using change as an impetus to move you further along and keep you in step with His ultimate big picture, you just may be experiencing a good ole retooling!

2

The Spiritual Band

I am a worshipper but not an artist, not a skilled musician before The Lord. What I need from those who lead me in worship, then, is that they take me where they have already been. I need for them to have been intimate with Jesus in their private hours so they can be my trusted guide into His presence. I need for them to be as prepared as a pastor would be for his sermon, as holy as the mystics of old, as gutsy as warriors need to be, and as eager for the journey as an adventurer setting off for the wild. Just take me there. That's all I ask. I can't get there on my own.

—Stephen Mansfield, Pastor, *New York Times* Best-Selling Author

Walk the Walk

The world is small. I'm in a security line today in South Africa, and standing next to me is a longtime friend from home with whom I've shared ministry and life over the past decade. He's a guy I can truly say walks the walk, spends himself on others, and has the same level of integrity and passion today as when I first met him. Seeing him had a very encouraging impact on my soul in a split second. It was grounding and reminded me that we're on the same team while traversing the planet for the glory of One, Jesus.

Have you ever known a person who started out one way and became someone you hardly recognized anymore in the midst of their pursuits and success? We really can forget where we come from and who we are! We need to be reminded that it's not about us when we're standing on the platforms and stages—in surrender to the One we claim to worship.

Our opponent knows well what it's about and is busy trying to disqualify us by any means, in order to keep us from the target goal. One way is by helping us become what we were never meant to be. If we lose sight of the call and the mission, we lose our effectiveness and saltiness.

I've known more stories than I care to know about artists, bands, musicians, singers, technicians, and the like. The saddest thing of all to me is when pride and ego convince any of us to believe our own press and we begin treating people differently. Can you imagine running into a friend whom you've been close with for a very long time, and he acts as if you didn't exist or he never knew you? What if Jesus treated us that way? Though we don't live in the fear of man, we should be concerned how our actions and words affect others.

Proverbs 27:21 says: "The refining pot is for silver and the furnace for gold, and a man is valued by what others say of him."

Here's where I'm headed with this: My friend Michael, whom I ran into on the other side of the world, is a man highly valued by those who know him. He doesn't have to ask to be given a place of influence or to be trusted, because that's just how he's known and who he is.

What do people say of you on- and offstage? My hope is that we raise the standard and be the kind of people and musicians who stand out because we remain consistent—no matter what. And that others would look on and say of us that we truly represent Jesus and His heart wherever we are.

As a band, don't just aim to be good or become known for your music alone; walk the walk of faith. Don't let success change who you are; God has always blessed those who remember Him!

Here are some tips:

1. Make it a point not to speak badly of others on your team, and don't say anything you wouldn't say in the presence of the one you're speaking about.

2. Treat everyone with the same respect and consideration—no matter his or her position.

3. Go out of your way to encourage every time you can.

4. Let others sing your praises and compliment you, receive it gracefully and humbly.

5. Value relationship over personal success or promotion, working hard and being diligent all the while.

6. Don't be a critic of others' talents and offerings in worship.

7. Never put down a team member in a corporate setting; share your issues honestly with him or her in private.

8. Be the same you on and off the stage.

9. Be devoted to God and worship Him, whether you get to play on the team or not.

10. Control your words and your temper. If you can't, know that it's not okay just to be that way, and work hard to change.

Make every effort for your life to be the testimony. It's for His glory that we give ourselves and our talents in worship. If we're not changed in the process of worshipping Him and becoming more like Him, then we're missing something. I challenge you to walk the walk. Don't just be a player!

More Than a Worship Band

I remember the first time I was hooked by music and cognizant of its power and influence. My family was visiting an aunt and uncle. They had a huge stereo—it took up a whole wall—and tons of records and 8 *tracks*! My uncle turned me on to the Beach Boys, and the song "In My Room" pierced me to the core. I knew then: this is my tribe, who I am, and what I must do (to be a musician, not a Beach Boy). Because I grew up in a musical and ministry family, I was also shaped by the songs from the Jesus music in the '60s that were inciting the young generation in Church. I cut my teeth on sing-a-longs, that's what we called praise and worship then. I have continued leading songs all of my career and ministry. My whole life, I've identified with spirituality and all kinds of music, yet I've had an innate passion and desire to sing not only in the Church but outside its walls too.

Many musicians and bands I meet serving faithfully in Churches all over the world also have a feeling there's more than song leading. There are quite a few well-known bands and artists that were once worship leaders or played in Church bands. It's a natural process as bands gel to form an identity, style, and uniqueness that urges them to move outward from the Church, become evangelistic, or just be who they feel they are. How great would it be if we didn't see this as a bad thing but helped release them as true disciples and worshippers to go make a difference—being salt and light in all kinds of arenas. My personal thought is that many of you are *genuinely* being led of God, but there is often a struggle to get there. That struggle generally comes with not knowing how to do it, being discouraged or unsupported by leadership, even fearing that it's wrong. It can't be wrong. Music from the Church has always had a presence in the world, and the Great Commission mandate is to go into the world, not withdraw or have nothing to do with it. We are to be in it, just not of it. Meaning, we do need to be in the Church.

My hope is to encourage Churches, leaders, and worship bands that feel this way, not to dismiss it as unholy or wrong. Let's not lose all the great artists and bands to the world because *it* gives them opportunity. Rather, let's prepare them and help them hit the target.

Speaking spiritually, it begins with simply being worshippers and a part of God's people, the Church. Within the Church community and family is where the greatest creativity should be commissioned, cultivated, nurtured, blessed, and sent out. If we can agree that the presence of God alone truly accomplishes His purposes, then that is our foundation. The goal is to produce worship and creative expression filled with His presence to carry His presence everywhere. I do think that lyrically, it means using more than just words we accept as standard worship lingo. If David sang about all aspects of his life unto God and it was real worship, surely we should too.

Worship leaders and bands should know their spiritual gifts and how to serve the Church with them. I don't mean talent but gifts—there's a difference. Gifts are meant to edify and build up. Talents are what we steward and invest. If we are busy serving with our gifts, we'll be productive spiritually for the Kingdom. There is much freedom to steward our talents. As a worshipper, all of life takes on the character and presence of Jesus that in and of itself causes effect wherever we go.

A natural by-product of a healthy Church is great art. If the commission is to go, then let's go to the world with our proclamations and expressions of God's truth, beauty, and glory.

So for the worship bands, songwriters, artisans, and singers within the Church who feel there's more, there is! God may lead some of you before kings and the masses and others to remain totally unseen or continue serving your local Church. The keys for me are to worship in spirit and truth, serve faithfully, and steward wisely. He uses faithful and surrendered lives.

Speaking practically, what do you do? You're a band that loves to lead worship, but you also have all these songs that don't fit congregational worship. Maybe some that do but aren't going anywhere or being heard. Or you have records you want to make, gigs you want to do, and so on. There are things you can do.

1. Take what you have, sharpen, focus, and prepare. Be diligent to ready
    yourselves both spiritually and musically, as an individual or a team. The
    world discerns quickly and knows a fake when it sees one, so be the best
    and most authentic person you can be. Lead. Don't follow how the world
    does it.

2. Don't wait for a record company, publisher, or investor to bankroll
    your vision. Just do it. Invest in a recording setup and hone your craft,
    document your songs and ideas, develop your sound, spend hours and
    hours and hours and more hours—doing the thing you do or want to do.
    If you're a songwriter, write many songs, and you'll just be getting started.
    Learn to record and demo as a band. Do as much as you can do yourself
    before pursuing help from others. Put your songs and demos together in a
    presentable fashion.

3. Through prayer, discern your target and get God's vision for you. Set your
    aim and goals around it. Never compromise your ability to steward what
    He's given you. Don't sign away or sell it for a platform. Platforms and deals
    don't give you a ministry. Ministry comes out of the fruit and integrity of
    your faith, life, and works. Know what God's purpose is for you. It won't just
    appear out of thin air, and no one else can tell you that. Without a clear
    vision, you won't accomplish very much or last long.

4. Trust God to promote you. Don't aim at stardom; aim to please God.
    Serving makes you a star with Him. Once you have tools such as CDs,
    demos, and so on, proceed humbly and honestly with those with whom
    God gives you opportunity and favor. Feedback and constructive criticism
    from a pro in any field can help but shouldn't define or defeat you. There's
    nothing wrong with sharing what you do and being who you are, but do
    so with integrity. If you are pursuing contacts, referrals are always better.
    Relationships count the most and shouldn't feel forced. If someone truly is
    in a position to help you with songs, projects, career, and so forth, you only
    want them to help if you can be healthily and equally yoked with them.
    Take time before you run ahead with what seem to be promising offers or
    opportunities; in all honesty, few of them ever are what they seem. Get
    some good, Godly counsel.

5. If you think you really want to pursue the worship or music industry,
    here's a wee bit of advice that won't cost you a thing: the sobering and

truthful reality is that there's a way things are done and you should become educated and aware. Count all the costs; be very certain that you are willing to do what it *will* take to go that way. I'm not picking on labels or artists here, so please hear me well. There is always a bottom line, an agenda on both sides, and a contract that spells things out clearly—though many enter in without having done due diligence, let alone sought God. Unfortunately, our word is sometimes the first thing out the window when it all goes south, but you signed the deal! The safest way to fulfill your call and use your God-given talents as a worship leader, band, or artist is: bloom where you're planted, do what you do, be faithful in the little, and live by God's wisdom. If as you're doing those things, *they* come knocking at your door with offers to help you, be sure it's a partnership that God can bless, and communicate everything well on the front end. Contracts can save friendships. I will go one step further to say that as believers, we should be people of covenant and promise and do what we say, even if it means we get the short end of the stick. Someone, somewhere, sometime will fail to live up to his or her end of the deal, and though we may have rights contractually speaking, that doesn't mean we're exempt from honoring what pleases God most in our relationships and dealings. Again, we've been given the power and gift of choice!

6.   Go for it—God can, and will, use you. What better than to have worshippers leading the way and impacting our world with God's presence? Dream, write, play, lead, sing—all to the glory of God.

What makes worship powerful and real is God's presence. What brings God's presence is humility and brokenness. What changes the reality of the world we're living in is God's Spirit working through us. Whether you're leading The Body of Christ in worship or standing in God's presence out in the world sharing your talents, it is worship. Let's not limit God to a contemporary worship box. Some of you are no less a worship band just because you play in unusual settings or your songs are about life. But if you are a worshipper, you are called to reflect Christ no matter where you play.

Conditioning

Fighter pilots train for many hours, repeating and re-repeating procedures and exercises in order to react instinctively in battle. They are conditioned to respond like a reflex. After a while, anything can become a habit and second nature if we put the necessary time into training; it's called conditioning.

How conditioned are we? As worship bands, we have our arsenal of familiar, simple, and "congregationally correct" songs. We know the routine. Become good at it and do it roughly the same every week. This is part of the role and takes a lot of time and effort for sure. But how much time do we put into training ourselves to go beyond the routine, to hearing and responding to God in worship? I'm not just talking about spontaneous worship, which for many is not even an option in a service. I mean engaging with God beyond the songs and outside the context of the service. Singing more than the standard worship vocabulary that we know so well, pouring out our hearts, and connecting with God. Showing up with no agenda or program to fit into, for the sole purpose of playing to an audience of one.

There's a place and time for being real and transparent before God. He will often move among the team, speaking not only to the leader but also to and through the other members. Giving us impressions or words to sing and pray. Taking us musically to places we've never been. After a while, we become conditioned to flow with Him. We grow in wisdom, discernment, and brokenness—becoming more driven to follow Him than to lead our own way. That is a place more teams need to go, although the service may or may not be the time and place to experiment in every case.

Thinking of the future of worship bands, we need to make more room for this kind of time. Readying ourselves to go beyond yesterday's move. We need His vision today. But it means setting aside the additional time. New songs, vision, and revelation are just some of the fruit that can come from it. As the Church, we should be preparing for a harvest that we already know is coming. Training and equipping, as Paul teaches. Serving in various ways, which is the heart of Jesus, and ever on the lookout for where He's taking us. We as leaders and teams are a part of that. Training and preparation is how we'll become sharp and useful. I know the realities and difficulties with it largely being a nonpaying deal already, but let's do what we can. Someone take the initiative, find a schedule that works; the rewards are worth it!

I realize there's a fine line between self-indulgence and responsibility. We can certainly take freedom to extremes and let our emotions carry us places God never meant us to go.

It is still true, however, that we are priests unto God, and we are to minister to Him first. If we spent an ounce of the time that many artists, athletes, and professionals do in order to become the best, we'd be leading the world in worship and having greater impact.

Many times we follow the world, looking at what it does as our guide and standard, especially musically. What it comes down to is taking the role as priests seriously and not just playing the gig. God inhabits the praises of His People, and it's the presence of His Spirit that makes the difference. Let's spend the needed time to dive into the Creator of all with our very best, bringing Him more than catchy songs and well-executed services. Try it!

1. Fix a time and place, as frequently as you can, to meet, pray, play, and *eat*. Bring in some encouraging teachers, mentors, leaders, and the like, to pour into you spiritually and musically. Treat this time as your boot camp. Trust God to bless and inhabit the time you've made for Him. Be consistent, and document songs, words, prayers, and so forth.

2. Share your heart and plan with your key leaders. Ask them to be praying about it. Invite them to share what God is showing them regarding worship, music, Church, life, and so forth. Be careful not to present it as something that will detract from your role as the worship band or leader but as something that will enhance it. Leaders: Make room for your team and avoid controlling or dominating this time. It should not be a fearful thing.

3. Make it a goal individually to prepare and to bring something to these meetings: songs, ideas, dreams, visions, and so forth. Read the Word, pray, and wait. Embrace the space and silence.

4. Find opportunities to serve as a band outside the normal service: an outreach, mission trip, or the like. Help a smaller Church; mentor others together. Build healthy relationships. It is a good outworking of what's happening internally during these times.

5. Keep it God centered, not self-indulgent. Be focused, stick to your allotted time, honoring everyone's time involved. Be committed, not flippant. It is an act of intercession and serves your entire body, not just the team.

Aim for Glory

This has been a year full of reminders already that life is a short stop on the way home. Recently we lost another friend and pioneer of Christian Music, Dana Key of DeGarmo and Key, who helped define the genre Contemporary Christian Music. Dana was a great player and singer and was still serving faithfully as a pastor. I packed up my car and set sail from Florida for Tennessee in '83, most likely listening to a cassette of DeGarmo and Key, arriving in Nashville an extremely passionate and driven seventeen-year-old. There are a good many people I've known in my journey on Earth, who, like Dana, now know the glory of Heaven and being with The Lord. Death is a part of living, but only the beginning of forever. It helps bring life into better focus and reminds us hopefully of what living is all about.

For a young and zealous musician, life was all about making my music—living the dream. I drove up and down Music Row in my late teens having it all mapped out, then life happened. Here's my little summary of the "road well graveled." For most musicians I know in Nashville, it started as an all-consuming quest fueled by an insatiable desire to play and create. Which leads to a thought: "I might actually be able to do this for a living," which leads to a roadway that you really don't expect to be as full of pain and reality as it truly is. Most won't be able to make a living doing it, and if you're not grounded in who you are to start with, the person you can become in the process is someone you may have never wanted to be. Our town is full of some very disappointed and unfulfilled creative people. It's illusive and dangerous when who we are depends on how well we do according to industry—or other's—standards.

A number of artists have reached the top, but what stands out as exceptional to me are the ones who've managed to keep their lives, marriages, and families intact. We spend a fair amount of words talking about how to do music and ministry. There's a seminar a minute for everything. I'd like to say a bit about the importance of maintaining life well. Not because I'm an expert, but because my own road is paved with lots of hard lessons. When I got to Nashville, I knew how to play and sing. What I was pretty clueless about was real integrity. Not only the "doing what you say" kind of integrity, but personal boundaries and character where it really counts. Choices I made early on affected me years later. It all adds up. What I've found is that God will let us run our paths, and we may even think we're doing it for all the right reasons, only to wake up one day and be way off course. Notoriety and success don't equal healthy ministry. A steady and faithful walk will keep us in for the long haul.

What good is it really to gain the world and lose the soul? What impact do we have if people know our names and music, but our lives are so full of holes that we live opposite from the way we are called by God to live? I read an interview with a well-known actress, who was asked about how great her life must be. She responded, "Yes, it's great, but I can't feel it!" If our issues, sins, pains, addictions, and so on drive us, then we'll drive ourselves crazy. No matter how great life may be, we won't feel it either, and the bad will overshadow the good. I spent years one season in deep depression not even knowing it, and was trying to give out and minister the whole time. We can do it so long, and then we run out of steam completely. In my case, a divorce and heart attack stopped me dead in my tracks. I lost some good time along the way, and thankfully we serve a redemptive God. I'm now remarried to my wife, which is a whole other miraculous story in itself! He turns our mourning into dancing without a doubt—I know it firsthand.

None of this is to make us feel worse about anything we deal with, I promise. Let's make our music be free and creative as God made us to be, but pay close attention to the condition of our lives and personal well being. We cannot sustain or keep up in our own strength alone. And unless we are able to contain the wine that God desires to pour into our wine skin, we'll bust eventually. We need to be made new every second of every day. That's why Paul made such a deal of choosing to walk in the Spirit. It's not a one- time thing. We have to choose it constantly, every single day.

God intends for His glory to shine through our lives. How we serve one another, what we choose to chase, and how we live behind the scenes determines whether or not it can or does. The good news is we don't have to be anyone but ourselves. God is very cool with us as we are already. We're going backward when we try to dress up and become someone we're not. Glory shines best through authenticity, purity, humility, and brokenness. If we want our talents and gifts to be used to the fullest, we must deal with our hearts first. Aim for glory!

Creative Struggle

Life goes by faster than I ever would've imagined. I'm on a tour in Canada right now with Matt Maher and Don Moen—quite the transgenerational worship experience I'll say, and it's great to be a part of it. I stepped outside the venue the other night for a breath of air. It was deafeningly silent in the country just outside of Calgary, the sun was setting down, and the air was nice and cool. I'm not that old, but I flashed back 25 years or so to the first time I came to Canada on a tour in my late teens. I was fearless and driven by a big dream and lots of passion. I loved God deeply but had a boatload of issues, which led to some bad choices that of course cost me, and hurt others along the way. I was running headlong into my bright future with a mountain of zeal but not yet seasoned by any real experience. A lot of life has passed since; in some ways I'm that same guy but in many ways not. Now I see clearly how God was directing my steps, bringing different people and experiences across my path to teach and help me beyond the moment I was in. One thing that's remained the same is my resolve to live life for Him, a choice I made and have never turned back from in spite of failures.

There are some things I wish I'd known when I hit the road right out of high school determined to be a "Christian artist." For one, this walk of faith and holiness is a process of being changed, not just about touring, recording, fun, and music. Being a Christian means we are being transformed, like The Word says, "from glory to glory." Even through our sins, mistakes, and hurts, He is sculpting and sanctifying us like vessels of clay—to hold what He desires to pour out through us. I also wish I'd known how important it is to make good choices all along the way. Time gets away fast, and enough bad choices add up to big messes. My parents and others tried to tell me, but I had to learn it for myself the hard way. At some point we have to reckon with our messes and the consequences of our choices. Though my biggest transformations have come through the muck and mire of my life for sure, not all of them had to be so hard—I can only blame myself for that.

Callings are hijacked every day by a savvy opponent who aims to derail us from God's best and steal what God has given to bring glory to Himself. I meet a lot of young bands and amazingly talented people all over the world who are passionate about their music and serving God. Unfortunately many who start the journey fall away or deviate from the original course, assaulted in every imaginable way through normal life issues. Addiction, adultery, depression, immorality, gluttony, anorexia, you name it. If we cannot manage our lives, then we don't stand much of a chance of living the destiny God has planned for us, and the enemy knows that.

It may seem fanatical or somewhat fairytale-like to some to hear this, but we really do live in a constant battle and have to fight to survive and thrive. It's not superspiritual to apply what the Bible teaches; it's very smart! Paul spent a lot of time reminding us where the battle really is, who it's against, and how to fight it. Read Ephesians. Being a follower of Jesus makes us a threat to hell, and the devil doesn't just roll over or go away. That shouldn't surprise us, but we are still shocked sometimes when the hard stuff arrives at our doorstep. That's when we are the most tempted to abandon our beliefs and faith. One of the key struggles believers have is blaming God when the bad comes, even though He clearly promised it would from the beginning. And a lot of it happens as a result of our own choices, though some of it He simply allows to happen to us, like Job. It's in the fire that we are tested and purified; we just don't like it because it hurts. But we'll see more victory over our issues when we trust God in the middle of the pain and struggle.

As musicians we need to grow up and learn to not only do our craft well as unto God, but also deal with the ever-present battle we're caught in. It's not enough to be cool or impressive. While we carry on business as usual pursuing our dreams, we and people in our family at large are losing the fight all around us—the lost are still lost, in need of the gospel. I think the hardest thing for creative people to do is understand calling versus talent. We're not called to do music per se, we're called to seek His Kingdom on Earth, reach the lost, do as He did while He was here, and build up the Saints. *A creative dream can either get in the way of a calling or help facilitate it.* So if we want be used creatively, we must know how to pray and stand in our faith, not letting our passion and excitement wane under pressure or fade to the background. Light shines best through darkness.

Ask yourself this: Am I chasing my dream or God? Am I tempted to revel in the limelight of the platform or surrendered in abandoned worship? Do I lose my faith and convictions when the darkness comes?

We need to understand the mission and let it drive the creativity. I highly encourage, no matter what age we are or role we play in whatever setting: Choose to live life for God no matter what comes. Default to His mandate for our lives and ministries. Let's not be casualties or led astray by our own egocentric ambition. That's how some of the most talented artists miss their mark. Guilt and condemnation paralyze, leading us into defeated places. Confession and repentance lead us to freedom and healing. That's where God wants us to live and that's where we're most effective in the battle.

A few suggestions:

1. Manage relationships well or they'll manage us; go the extra mile to keep them healthy. Resolve friction, conflict, envy, or division, as lovingly, selflessly, and expediently as possible. A band or vision will only last as long as the relationships.

2. Find ways to focus creative energy and passion on serving others and helping our mates succeed as often as we can.

3. Walk humbly—not proudly like a diva, believing our own press. We're just as human as the rest and need the grace and mercy of God just as much.

4. Be serious about our spiritual life and health. We don't just get it and grow by osmosis. If we ignore all the safeguards and truths meant to help protect us, we'll forfeit blessing—leaving ourselves wide open to have our calling hijacked; it happens all the time.

5. If we find ourselves going the wrong way, turn around, redirect. God is merciful beyond our understanding and always patient. Don't spiral down into condemnation and guilt over sin and issues, but deal with them by getting into the light and walking in the safety of community.

Discover Your Band

Being a visionary band/artist is harder than it seems. Any group of musicians can put a band together, even sound good, but few really lead or have lasting impact or testimonies worth noting. One reason great athletes command such deep respect I think is that they normally spend a lifetime preparing, working, and training for their dreams. Not too many overnight sensations in the sports world. Though good marketing and money can possibly make you a star in music, it can't give you the stuff of legend, because legends take a long time to make and are normally born through pain and preparation. Even more so Godly legacies.

It is a privilege and honor to serve the God of the Universe. As His chosen beacons in a dark, fallen world, we are entrusted with a message that affects and changes reality everywhere it lands, so we want to represent Him well in everything we do. It's important to remember daily that we don't fight against flesh and blood but rulers and principalities of darkness at work against us in this world. We're always shocked when others fall from grace and make mistakes, but truth is, it could just as easily be any of us. Our opponent is well acquainted with our issues and weaknesses and is patient to undermine God's work in us. What that has to do with being visionary is we have a choice when it comes to pursuing dreams and passions, to follow God or the way of the world. Sadly, as Christians in music, we sometimes look to heroes and stars for inspiration and direction more than to our God. Yet the only hope we have against our adversary is being filled with God's Spirit and seeking His Kingdom first.

We work very hard to become good bands musically, maybe not as hard to be healthy and alive spiritually. My challenge wherever you are in your journey is to build your musical dreams and visions on a good foundation, one that can be blessed, sustained, and promoted—should God desire it. It's backward from the way the world music business works, maybe even some Churches. The point is, we are living and breathing *for such a time as this* and want to be effective and fruitful. The creativity is no problem for God, and if we focus our plans around Him, the music can reach its full potential.

Some steps to laying a good foundation include: identifying who we are as followers and worshippers of Jesus; knowing our spiritual gifts, as described in 1 Corinthians 12; surrendering and stewarding our talents well. Once we understand and can articulate who we are and what we do, we can make plans and take necessary steps. Whether a worship band, pop band, country band, or whatever, our first commitment is to God's plan and glory being revealed in our lives. The music is secondary. Since God will not share His glory, we can't expect to be useful from a Kingdom perspective if we choose to do it our own way. It always costs dearly to compromise Godliness for earthly pursuits.

Instead of waiting to be discovered, do now what you say you want to do. Even as a band, you can serve and make a difference. If you're waiting for someone to *give you a chance or a big break*, stop waiting and go do. Opportunity usually comes when we are busy with the work already or serving where we can today. Having a vision is an imperative first step. It doesn't have to be completely figured out, just needs to be present to avoid wandering aimlessly—expecting others to do for us what God has given us to do ourselves. That vision should come from hearing God regarding what is important to Him and specific for us. Hard as it may be to listen and hear, He is always speaking and will guide if we follow.

A mistake made over and over with often tragic outcome is giving *our* vision over to be controlled by another. Usually because we think it's going to further us or our careers, but it's also sometimes out of trust. Not that it's wrong to trust, but no other human being should have ultimate control over or dictate your vision. By that I simply mean, if God has given us something specific to do, we shouldn't sign it over or give it away, since it's ours to steward. We alone are responsible and accountable to God for what He gives us, and so should guard and protect a vision. You cannot expect a company, Church leader, your mom, your dad, or anyone to do it for you. God will honor your diligence and faithfulness.

Can you say with confidence that you know what you're called to do? There's a lot of freedom to create and express what God has put in us through our talents. They are for His pleasure above all, and we also get to enjoy them, which is great. But what we're called to is the mandate of Christ in Matthew 28: 18–20.

If you want to be released onto a world stage, into a harvest field wide and deep, first discover God's vision for you, then for your music!

Passion and Greatness

Passion and greatness are inspiring, and people are drawn to both. As a ship is steered by a rudder, we are certainly steered by passion. "Where your treasure is, there will your heart be also" (Matt. 6:21). Greatness isn't a given and is relative to the standard of measure that we use. There are some artists that have achieved greatness, and undoubtedly a very focused passion is what in part led them there. What I call great, you could easily regard as *not* so great. So whose standard do we rely on and esteem most? If I tallied up a few artists I think are great now versus when I was younger, the list would look very different. Most I would still love, and I might even use the word *great* in conjunction with their names. But over time, what stands out are the few who've truly laid down their own greatness in order to be used for God's glory. That's because the glory road is a harder road to take, and it requires sacrifices that go completely against the grain of creative people. However, glory shines bright through the one fueled by a passion that is bridled and fully surrendered to God.

In the early days of rock, music was by no means technically, sonically, or musically perfect. Guitars were out of tune, tempo drifted like the wind, vocals weren't autotuned to perfection, no beat detective, no cutting and pasting, and so forth. Yet the passion and raw expression was unquestionable and has proven for some to be timeless. In an age in which technology rules and is more accessible than ever before, one thing is still true: you need the passion! Without it you don't really have much. You have to create and capture the essence of something great for it to really become great.

There was a time when record labels took years to develop their artists and their music. It wasn't as easy as just sticking any- and everyone who could play or sing in front of people. Long before artists were seen, they were heard. All the greats started somewhere, and spent time honing and defining their passions into what we now know them to be. It didn't happen overnight, and it did cost them something. With worship music now being a genre and career choice, there's much more opportunity and possibility of foregoing proper development. For the world, development is more about the music, image, and market worthiness. For Christians, it is more about the heart, so to follow the world's example is not our way. The criteria to be an artist, whatever title we wrap around it—even a worship artist—should be about the quality and fruit of a life and ministry.

In my mind there are two roads creative people can run down. You can "go your own way" as Fleetwood Mac put it, or you can do it God's way. Many misguided Christians have mistakenly attributed their success and fame to God, adding His name to their ministries and businesses as if that alone legitimizes whatever they do. What's wrong with that is that what God asks and requires of us is in many ways backwards and in direct opposition to our own passion. This doesn't mean He hasn't given us the passion in our hearts, but the fullness is not attained by going our own way, doing our own thing, and being whatever we want or dream. It's best summed up this way: "Seek Ye first the kingdom of God and His righteousness and all these things will be added unto you" (Matt. 6:33). It's the righteousness part we misunderstand or glide over if we're not careful. We are not called to fame or riches, though we may have them and God does allow them. We are called to a priesthood and a lifestyle of holiness.

Not many bands set out to be priests. Many do have a history of some kind in the Church but don't seem able to maintain an obvious or dedicated passion to bring glory to God. At some point usually, it becomes about their glory, whether intended or not. I want to be clear that I am not picking on one side or the other; we are all human. Christians love, idolize, promote, exploit, and crucify their heroes just the same—read the history books! What I am suggesting is: many whom God gifted and called have missed the road entirely, though musically they may be greatly revered.

The beauty of art and music is that no one rule covers or applies to all creativity. It is a free gift from the Creator, who simply asks that we freely give it back to Him from our hearts. There is a lot of freedom involved. At some point, because we have free will, we have to choose whose glory we are going to invest in and pursue. For bands or artists to set their aim on being known or discovered can be a distraction and become an engulfing pursuit. The more you chase and pursue, the more you become responsible for and feel you have to maintain. That pressure alone has driven many way off course from where they started. I'm not talking about the pursuit of a passion in the sense that you do all you can to create and improve. Striving for excellence is good; believing you have to be on a platform to really impact is not. By all means make your music as great as you can make it; focus and be diligent to steward the talent you have. But don't let the talent lure you away from the calling of God on your life. It is not the end but a means to express devotion and love to and for God. God is passionate about people and their souls. The goal is always the same for Him: to seek and save the lost, commune with his people, and receive our lives as acts of worship.

So if you are trying to find a vibe, a sound, an image, a look—here's what I pray. Be creative, be yourself, be diligent; but above all, know, understand, and commit to being who you're called to be first. And be able to articulate what that is. Don't wait for others to tell you what you need to say and do in order to succeed and fill the role of Christian artist; get it for yourself. God is not silent and is still speaking. When you're on the stage, it needs to be about more than just your music. This doesn't mean it all has to be *worship* music either, just don't be nebulous or naïve about the calling.

Passion is a gift, greatness is a noble and worthy pursuit, but glory makes the difference. Aspire to live a passionate revolution centered on God's kingdom and glory. Live sacrificially, serve the world, walk humbly with Him, and trust him to thrust and propel you into spheres of influence and platforms as He sees fit.

3

Band Relationships

Being created in the image of God, we were created for relationship. God never intended for us to "go it alone!" Ultimately a successful ministry team or band will be characterized by God honoring relationships between its members and by their resulting trust in each other. To relate effectively with each other we must want to learn how to be better listeners—listening involves patience, openness, and very importantly the desire to understand. In relationships where there will be mutual respect, there will necessarily be the need for two very important ingredients: truth and love. Truth told in love enables us to grow, produces change, and brings healing. "…and so speaking the truth in love, we will in all things grow up into Him who is the Head, Who is Christ…" Eph. 4:15.

There should be no "superstars" in God's work—there should only be members of one Body working together in unity to form an effective team— each performing their special roles using their unique gifts to complement each other.

—Rolf Weichardt, National Director, Youth for Christ South Africa; Worship Leader and Team Trainer

Band in Conflict

In seminars and conferences around the world, I hear from leaders and band members many of the same questions regarding how to deal with conflicts. So I thought I'd spend some lines on the subject.

One thing that should set Christian musicians apart from the rest is how we handle conflict, our attitudes in general really. In past articles, I've spoken of how we need to approach all of life and our music as servants. If you want to stand out, learn how to manage conflicts well. In worship, it's not that we can't be human with our stuff, but that the bar is higher for those who strive to reflect a humble and Christlike spirit.

What-to-do-if list:

1. There's a weak player in the band?

   Fire them! No, actually someone should make it his or her personal aim to help them improve. Make constructive suggestions in private. If they are a hindrance—or totally incapable of keeping up with the band—the leader should pull them aside, privately speaking honestly with them about their weaknesses. Make every possible effort to grow them or direct them to private instruction with a goal to include them later on. You may also want to start a farm team, or B team, to mentor younger players. Offer alternatives and cultivate relationship in a positive and helpful way. Don't talk behind their backs or be rude to them.

2. There's a performer personality?

   We all bring our stuff with us into a band scenario and platform. The good news is that God is aware of it and lovingly deals with us. We aren't heart police, but we can help encourage those who love the moments in the limelight or in the lead. Whatever you do, don't bash them. If you see something that would help them, or if you have advice to give, be sure you've prayed and that it comes from a healthy, loving place. Then go to them personally, and don't take two or three to back you up. As a rule, with relational and character issues, don't discuss it with others before you go to the person. Always ask yourself how you'd like to be treated!

3. One member shows up late consistently for rehearsals and arrives just in time to play for the service?

   Dock their pay! (*You mean you're getting paid?*) That would be one way to expect more from band members and get it, but most are not paid in Churches. That's a whole other article! Again, commitment to the team is important, but you have to build your program based on what the reality is for the entire band. Find the happy medium for schedules, jobs, families, and the like. Make clear what expectations are. For leaders, that does mean considering and including your band in the process. If members then fail to adhere to requirements and schedules, remind them that everyone agreed when they signed on, and it's unfair for some and not all to be faithful. It is an issue of priorities, responsibility, and ultimately character, no matter what. It may take only one band member expressing his or her frustration, feelings of unfairness, or inconsideration with that person to shape them up a bit. There are extenuating circumstances, and certainly the worship team isn't more important than family or spouses. Weigh all of your priorities, count the cost before you commit, and be people of your word!

4. One band member dominates and controls or has a contagiously bad attitude?

   There's a new one for you, *give that one a spanking*! It happens, and more than it should, that one becomes the self-appointed critic, judge, opinion, leader, and so forth. Let's start with this: if you do have a leader, then you are responsible to submit to them as unto God and give your best. One thing is certain; the dominating personality can dictate and drive the entire situation, causing more division and frustration among your team if you allow them to. Here again, if it's problematic, the leader should take the initiative and correct that person one on one. Also be willing to part ways if they don't change the bad behavior, even if they are the best thing since sliced bread on their instrument! Don't procrastinate whatever you do; deal with it, but do it lovingly.

5. Your leader doesn't allow you much freedom?

   That's a tough one. There's always the issue of having to follow and support when you don't like it. That's life. There is a way, however, for leaders and band members to work together that produces the best and happiest situations. You first have to choose whether or not you can support your leader. If you can't, find somewhere else to give your talents. If you can, don't complain and gripe about those things you don't like! Learn, listen, and view this as an opportunity to serve and grow. There will be other opportunities for you to lead or express your freedom. Having said that, leaders, it's not a bad idea to let your band participate and flow naturally—as bands can do. Build on that, discuss ideas, consider members' opinions. Try going in different directions and leaving space for exploration in worship. Defer at times to the talents you share the platform with, and practice that exploration and freedom in your rehearsals. The more each person feels valued and included, the better he or she will play and serve, and the more freedom there will be.

6. Your leader's style is dated or the music selection is boring?

    Bring your ideas and suggestions to your leader to see if they're responsive and open to help or improvement. Sometimes they are not the most gifted, but they may be the most willing. Honor them, let them know you do support them and want what is best for them. Have listening parties with your team, discuss what everyone likes, and bring musical selections, CDs, music, new songs, and so forth to try. You always play better when you like the material and style. Find the common ground and be flexible. A good leader knows their own limitations and surrounds themselves with those who improve them, and are in many cases better. That brings up the issue of humility; it's hard for some. In some cases they are the way they are, and they're unwilling to change—or just don't know how. You can't always have the most ideal or desirous situation. Know your role and be willing to play your part no matter what with a good attitude!

7. Your leader isn't prepared or disciplined and it costs you time and frustration?

    Don't mess with them; they're God's anointed! *Well even the anointed need work.* First of all, we all lead someone and something in our lives and will grow in those skills mainly when given opportunities to rub elbows with others. That gets messy. We will continuously have to step up to the plate in areas of discipline, communication, and preparation. It is common sense that the leader be able to provide leadership for the band. It's not the hard and fast rule, but it sure makes it easier if you have your songs, charts, reference CDs, and so forth ready for your team. Everything goes better and faster, and then you're not pawning off your responsibility by neglect or laziness. Sometimes it will take you as members sharing truthfully with your leader how important the opportunity and your time are. It's about mutual respect and consideration for both the leader and the team. Once schedules and commitments are made, hold each other accountable, even the anointed! Say something, don't just brew on it till you blow up one night. Leaders: don't make excuses, and do your best to lead by example.

8. You have a personal conflict with a bandmate or leader?

The Word is a standard, even for rock and roll worship bands. *Do all things in unity, without grumbling or disputes; speak truthfully in love.* Always go right to the source of a problem, and don't turn it into a family affair. More problems and strife could be avoided if we did that and truly treated others the way we'd want to be treated. The tongue is a fire, so be careful not talk too much. Do the responsible albeit difficult thing, and confront your conflicts; just leave your anger and attitudes at home. There is a best way, and it's the high way; choose that way!

9. You have to dismiss a band member?

Take them to Starbucks first! Coffee covers a multitude of hardships (1 Tom 1:3). Well it happens, and it's no fun. Honesty is a must. Kindness and love really help, but at some point, you have to break the news that it's not working. Offer helpful suggestions, and be truthful about the reasons. Build them up as far as you can, yet be clear, and don't use too many words. Don't be confusing or contradicting. Don't use others' words as support or ammunition against them; keep it first person. Do your best to maintain a good relationship. If they do run off in a huff, be sure you've done all you can to be right, Godly, loving, and holy in your dealings with them. If it's not a long-term dismissal, specify a rest period to evaluate or work on issues, skills, and so forth.

10. You have to choose one player over another?

Do so carefully, and don't burn the bridge with the other player. Find other ways to include them or sub them in sometimes; rotate. As a leader, you cannot please or include everyone. Just do your best in your situation, and aim to win friends. It's also good to avoid letting posts become too heavily guarded by one person, causing competition among your team. Build a team mentality, where everyone roots for the other players and supports the whole; that's part of leading and good leadership!

11. You're in the band and overworked?

I think it's good, period, to take seasons of rest from the platform to just engage in worship personally. Even though you may fear losing your spot or not being called again. If you can't serve in whatever capacity with your priorities—and life—intact, it will only lead to bigger issues or burnout. Trust God to work in spite of others' expectations. Take breaks, and clearly communicate with your leader the reasons. You alone are responsible for what God leads you to do. Others must respect that and deal with it. Just be sure to honor your commitments and your word. Be careful not to overcommit yourself or allow yourself to be abused or used by an overzealous and superpassionate leader. Better you keep healthy and determine your own boundaries at the start!

12.   Your leader is a controller?

Here again, you do have a choice of whom you are going to submit to. Good leaders evoke followers without having to control. In my opinion, controllers squelch the life of a team. I think we need more faithful friendships, which will confront and exhort in love. But it can often mean a parting of ways, which prevents many from dealing with it. The leadership gifting in the Church is meant to serve and build up, not lord over and control. I don't believe we should just accept controlling behavior, but the way you confront it is very important! Forming a posse is not the right way. You may also have to go to the primary leader of your Church if the controller doesn't see the problem or refuses to deal with it. But I encourage first going to the person and being honest. Pray for your leader. Ask God to give you a real heart for them. Know what The Word says about leadership, and hold one another accountable to it. That is our standard; anything else or less is not of God. Do whatever you do in humility and love. Leaders: I strongly encourage you to ask God to reveal any control in you and be willing to face it if it's an issue. See it not just as "you've got a problem," but that you're a target for that spirit, and it has been a primary weapon used to hinder leaders throughout Church history.

I'll leave you with this, some of the best advice I have heard (Phil. 2:3–5): "Do Nothing out of selfish ambition or vain conceit, but in humility consider others better than yourselves. Each of you should look not only to your own interests, but also to the interests of others. Your attitude should be the same as that of Christ Jesus."

Tactfully Correct

I have a dear friend, Rick, who is without a doubt the most gracious and tactful man I know. I could say something and clear a room; he'll say the same thing and earn a friend. It's a gift. It's also something he chooses. I realize from years of knowing him that he is consistently the gentlemen and servant, no matter what the deal is. I watch in utter amazement as he glides through tough situations or handles hard cases with grace and tact. More than any other, he has challenged me to let go of my way or my need and see the greater picture.

More feelings are hurt and relationships marred by poorly handled moments than by almost anything else. Nothing has helped me more as a musician than learning to consider first how important my contribution really is before blurting it out; even still I don't always do it!

Since a band is comprised of a group of uniquely different people, how you relate may well determine how long you or the band lasts. There are those you want to be around and those you don't; which one are you? Wherever you land, here are some helpful tips.

1. Know your own tendencies and weaknesses, and counteract them with opposite actions. In my case, it's easy to lead or take charge when needed, but it's not always best, or my place. So I ask first: "Whose place is it?" I may reframe my suggestions as questions to the one in charge, or I excuse myself from taking the role that isn't mine anyway and just chill out or go for a coffee—whatever it takes! Even if what I know could help, it's often better unsaid, and sometimes it only complicates the situation.

2. Choose to be encouraging not discouraging; it absolutely never hurts! Being a Southern boy, I know that "Bless his/her heart" really means "Look out, you're about to get an earful!" Cloaking truth isn't helpful, but criticism isn't either when spoken wrongly. Even if someone isn't up to par musically or is hard to get along with, be a friend first and encourage the positives you see, which usually earns the right to be truthful later in a better context.

3. Guard your own emotions and feelings. Many times we take things too personally, even if not aimed at us directly or intentionally. If a misguided word or even truth comes your way, decide ahead of time it's not gonna

rock your world or shut you down. If we're always threatened by it, we make it hard on those around us to ever know what to say or do.

4. Recognize and avoid controlling. Being a songwriter and living in Nashville, where cowriting is a normal thing, has helped me be more openhanded with my ideas. For many, the natural inclination is always to steer something the way they see it needs to go or be. But in a band, there are other important voices to consider that add to the overall result, and we either learn to value them or make them feel devalued. We can be who we are without imposing or dictating.

5. Use fewer words. I'm a talker; no *amens* please! I'll go around the trees and through the woods in effort to have you fully understand me. Note to self: the deer in the headlight stare is a good sign it's time to zip it! I am better now at being my own editor. With confrontation, the more you say, sometimes the worse it becomes. In live/worship situations, time is of the essence, so less is more.

What's great about my friend Rick is that everybody loves him, wants to work with him, play music with him, because he makes everyone around him feel important and valued. Being tactful and erring on the side of grace will help us all, especially in worship, where it's not about us anyway.

Inclusiveness Versus Healthiness

It's no fun to be left out; who likes it? So where is the line between including everyone who wants to be a part of your team and maintaining and promoting healthiness? I don't know that there's a secret formula or standard that works across the board, but I do have some thoughts.

Here are a few principals from the Bible that help as guidelines; I'll summarize for time's sake: Unity commands a blessing; worship is for God alone, not men; self promotion is not good; considering others more important than yourself is important; stewardship is a must; and God values relationship, integrity, humility, and a broken spirit. He also desires that we do all things from the heart, for Him.

It's common and natural for the creative personality to desire to be a part of what's going on and not be overlooked. For many it's about having a genuine heart to serve and stewarding their talents well, but for some it's the desire to be seen, noticed, or identified with their gifting. Two things are true here: God wants us to serve with our spiritual gifts and talents, but He also considers priesthood a holy thing. We can't forget or dismiss the latter just because it's also true that He's gracious and merciful. Who really knows what worship in spirit and truth looks like, but surely it has to start with purity of heart and reality-based living before God and with others.

So how do we include without compromising purity and integrity? Purity of heart is not something we can judge; God does that. We can't know the heart of another fully and are not called to police others. We each come to serve and yet still have issues. Thankfully, God sees the heart! What I encourage is some kind of process that's unique to you, where you bring in those who want to participate through relationship first. This provides a training and preparation stage to grow friendship and trust in leadership. Lay your vision and expectations out clearly, find out what prospective team members desire in worship, why they want to be involved on the team, how committed they are, and so forth. If you approach the worship ministry with a "come one, come all" mentality, you will end up with more than you really want, need, or bargained for. I understand that for some, it may mean going without versus having the wrong leadership. You are standing in a holy place, not merely leading songs. I'll say here again though: God uses the willing and broken, which will usually confound our wisdom. He often chooses the one we don't see and historically anoints who He pleases. The key is not control but reverence. And being diligent to do all you can to preserve and promote an attitude of holiness and awe among the team. Servant leadership is the model I see that works best, and humility is not only required, it is necessary.

Another suggestion is that you zero in on building a healthy team both spiritually and musically. Don't become exclusive, but do guard against bad attitudes and those who bring in or cause division. It's not wrong to say no when it applies. Leadership requires making those kinds of decisions, and yes, grace applies when you make mistakes, which you will. If you have the need to have more than one team, do it, but not at the expense of maintaining health. I realize that every situation is different. If there is a team with more skill and another that's just not up to par, it's not wrong to let them both be who they are. You can nurture both, and there's no need to establish one as better than the other; both are good.

It's important to remember: we are priests unto God first, then servants to his people. We are also leaders, and that involves modeling. You will reproduce what you live out and model. It's nearly impossible to find one model that always works, except Jesus. Apply all you can from His lifestyle and teachings, and develop a ministry based on that first. From there, if you are truly surrendered to Him, walking in humility, and leading as a servant, you will attract many but also have the wisdom to oversee and lead in a Godly way. To team members: I encourage always trusting God to open doors and proceeding with open hands, not as if you have the right to be included in something because it's the Church. It's a hard place for leaders to be in when it comes to overseeing the ministry of worship. Be patient and prayerful, check your heart and attitude, and be willing to serve even in the smallest of ways.

The worship time shouldn't be a self-indulgent ministry time. Let's draw attention to our Creator and love each other in the process. In reality it's both: inclusiveness and healthiness.

Are You Easily Offended?

A Brother offended is harder to win than a strong city, and contentions are like the bars of a castle.

—Proverbs 18:19

I was having a conversation last night, and the question was asked why some worship bands and ministries have an air of arrogance surrounding them. An attitude of "We are it, "This is our gig," or "It's our time." Also, there are many who want to be on the team or play more regularly and seem get their feelings hurt often because they're not being asked to.

Part of the problem to me is that we are too focused on the main worship event and preoccupied with being involved with it. It's almost like there's an unspoken rule that you're only effective and being used if you're on the stage during the key meetings. There's a bottleneck of creative talent, all aiming to get out of the same chute. In truth, the heart that's pure should always trust and wait for God to bring the opportunities. In the meantime, we should be busy about the needs and opportunities already staring us in the face. Even if our hearts are perfectly right and humble, we may be overlooked, and yet we're still responsible personally to not be easily offended and to steward what we're given.

To be clear, I don't think most of us set out to control or abuse the worship platform, but it happens in and through us all. Any offense can turn into a breach or bad attitude. Any familiar comfort zone can, and will, be challenged at some point. The gig will always expire, and all are replaceable. There is some way we can each participate and be used, but it may not be the way we're hoping or aiming for. It may take time to get there, and it may never be on a stage. The real question is: Are we okay with that? Do we trust God to promote and make a way for us or not?

In the music world, it's normal for players to vie for position and protect their gigs. It happens in all walks of life actually; it's the way we humans are. Christians, who are imitators of Jesus, should strive to be different from that. We should be happy when another gets the opportunity or praise; we should be looking for others to champion and encourage. If we step on stage having stepped over others to get there, what does that say about the quality and integrity of the worship we're bringing, when at the very heart of worship should be humility and purity? Even if we're not vying for a place, it is true that we all avoid and neglect things closest to God's heart along the way to worship. The one thing each of us does have the opportunity to control is our attitude.

How practical is this for the band? The hardest things you will likely do as a player are learn to be selfless, serving, humble, grateful, encouraging, helpful, faithful, preferring, and so forth. In every situation that I've personally experienced, the good attitude wins and is most often asked back. It's a small thing but is the most powerful witness. It always pleases God when his people choose the high road, to be overlooked or offended without taking recourse. Watch VH1's *Where Are They Now*, and you can trace most breakups back to selfishness, pride, and seriously offended people. Talent alone is not enough.

Are you aiming to worship with all your might, play skillfully, please God, and serve? Then choose now not to take offense. Try it the next time a leader or player suggests what he or she thinks you should be playing or doing. In the ultimate scheme, it has little to do with the music and all to do with the character of Jesus in us. Even the creative genius needs to see with new eyes, and hear with new ears, the heart of God.

Who's the Leader

In most cases it's obvious who the leader is. I am asked the following questions a lot: Does the musical leader have to be the worship leader? Can a band member be the musical or spiritual leader if he or she is not the lead singer? Is the lead singer always the leader? Every situation is different, and normally there's one who stands out as being the most capable leader. If your Church has hired or appointed one as the leader, then they're the leader, even if they're not the most qualified. I've said before: it's important to follow and listen to your leader; that's a biblical and Godly responsibility of every one of us. What the best leaders do, however, is find those better than themselves and help them shine in their strengths.

To clarify, I'll subdivide areas of worship leadership into spiritual, musical, song leader, worship leader, administrator.

> *Spiritual Leadership*: Gifts of leadership, as outlined in Ephesians 4, are given to the Church to build up and equip. A spiritual leader will have natural strengths that lean toward one or more of these gifts, so it's not the talent but the gift that makes the leader spiritual. God gives to certain people a unique bent and concern for the spiritual condition and well-being of others, also a deep sense of what pleases Him in worship.

> *Musical Leadership*: Competence, skill, experience, knowledge, and talent make up a good musical leader. Though it can be learned and refined through education and/or practice, it can also be a natural talent and ability, which some have more of than others. The musical leader is the one whom the band depends on most. Typically he or she carries the songs and provides the stability and foundation. Often it's the key leader, but not always.

> *Song Leader*: In most cases, it's one person who leads the songs, and he or she may or may not be the worship leader. I have seen the leader change every other song. In any case, I call the song leader the point person or lead singer of a particular song. It's a rule, to me anyway, that the band supports the singer who's carrying and delivering the song lyrically, thus making him or her the song leader. For the instrumental worship band, it's the musicians themselves or a band leader.

> *Worship Leader*: This title means different things to different people. I had a young teenage friend and worship leader say recently, "I've noticed something that's different about certain worship leaders. It goes way beyond talent, ability, and whatever else. It's like a special power that not everyone has." He went on to use the word *anointing*. I would say that while I don't see "worship leader" listed as a spiritual gift, there are for sure some who seem more able to lead others into worship. It does seem to have to do with the heart more than skill, though some have both, and anointing is certainly something God does, not us. The worship leader is the one who is keenly, humbly, and earnestly seeking God and ministering

to Him while leading others into worship. Oddly enough, it's not always the lead singer, but most commonly.

Administrator: In most bands, there's an organizer/administrator type who pulls it all together. Again, it's a gifting; see 1 Corinthians 12:28. Sometimes it's the worship leader, or maybe it's the worship secretary. Whoever is handling the details behind the scenes, he or she is the administrator.

The reason I've subdivided these aspects of leadership is to help you identify who the leader is among you. It doesn't need to be a daunting thing or a threat to the rest. What's important is that there is leadership in your band; otherwise, artist types can notoriously flounder.

To me the worship-leading ministry is a holy and reverent thing that God didn't give to just anyone to steward throughout history. He set aside a whole tribe to be devoted to ministry unto Himself and service in the temple on behalf of his people. Where I see the rub happen is when we give place to talent over leadership and stewardship. Some with the heart aren't as rich in the talent department but are the more qualified leaders. So leadership is key to bringing these together and setting the standards of holiness and excellence as we serve.

The given is that you are responsible to follow the leadership provided by your Church. If you don't have that but want to find it, then start by identifying the key spiritual leader of your band and affirming and supporting him or her as such. Determine who is the most capable and willing to be the musical leader, let the natural organizer do that job, and let God point out the natural worship leader in your midst. It may be more than one. If so, make room. The key is that it's not a position to control or own, nor is it about performing for people. In truth, the whole band is in a sense the worship leader, with someone at the helm. It's not uncommon for one person to be all of the above—in fact, it's great if that's so. Don't be scared to share the responsibilities as they relate to your gifting. When I read about the priests in the Old Testament, what stands out is that there were many of them, all with different gifts and talents, committed to the same purpose!

Leaders are often the ones who are simply willing to do the job and take initiative. If we're not careful, we'll choose the most obvious or one with the highest musical qualifications alone and miss the best worship leader. I always go back to King David. He was the runt of the litter and most likely to have been overlooked by humanity but was seen with the eyes of God through a prophet, chosen, and anointed king. Worship was just the way he lived his life; that made him a man after God's heart and the best leader, as he valued God's glory and will above all.

If you're a worshipper, then you're also a worship leader to some degree. The marks of a good worship leader are brokenness, honesty, and humility. Whoever the leader is, he or she should demonstrate these qualities and characteristics. God gives grace to the humble but opposes the proud. To desire to lead is noble and good but comes with responsibility. We need God's wisdom to do it best.

Sum of the Parts

One of my favorite songs from way back has a line in it that says this: "Love is choosing/ Love is losing/Love is finding when you give it all away." It's not easy for many musicians to give away. By that I mean there's a "protect yourself" mentality that seems to come with the artist/musician personality and wiring.

In my town, one of the first questions asked is "What do you do," or "What have you been doing?" What that means is what do you play, who are you playing with, and what are you working on? For an ungrounded or overly insecure person, identity can become so tied to what we do that we have no idea who we really are. If we don't have something of weight or excitement to answer back with, we can feel small by comparison.

When I moved to Nashville at 17, I found myself living on Music Row, surrounded by others' successes and overwhelmed by "The Dream." The lure and temptation was immediate to prove myself and showcase what I do. The sobering reality was that many around me could *do* it better. One of the first things God began to reveal to me was that my talent is not what I am called to first. There'll always be others more talented, and what He has asked of me is to use it for His glory above my own. I decided a long time ago that I wanted to learn to give it away versus living in a constant state of anxiety over who I'm *not*. For our happiness and well-being to be determined by comparison to any other is not at all what God intended, and is actually a sin that we sometimes tolerate and accept as normal.

I've just spent a week in the studio with some friends carving up songs and arrangements. It's a very fulfilling process, and though tedious work, worth it. Here's how it went. We'd start with the song, throw it out there, and then begin chiming in with our ideas for the arrangement and parts. There wasn't a dictator among us. Everyone's voice was heard, and at the end of the day, the results were beautiful. The sum was greater than the individual parts for sure. Whether our ideas were used in full or part, we were all a part of the process and experience. We'll likely not remember who thought of what anyway; the blessing was just being part of the family effort.

Not every session has gone that way. I've also spent the entire time sweating, wondering if what I'm doing is good or not, and being inhibited because there's a better player involved or thinking another's contribution was way better than mine, and on and on it went. The hot seat is no fun to be in; you're very much in the spotlight and under scrutiny. So the experience is not always great. More than once, I've left thinking maybe I should take up cattle farming in the Swiss Alps; I have friends there.

Have you ever been championed by someone? There's nothing like encouragement, especially from someone you deem better than you are at the very thing you do. Though I am still very human and selfish, my tune started changing when I met some older, wiser players and heroes that lived out a "give it away" lifestyle. They exuded a whole lot more peace than I'd ever known, because they were okay with who God made them to be. There was no secret to conceal or protect, no threat to their talent or ability or position to prove or maintain. Living with a fear that you're not enough *just as you are* is a perpetual misery.

We are a diverse tribe; I'm amazed how many incredibly talented people I know and meet regularly. It's like looking at the sky and seeing the countless stars: you can't keep track. All are uniquely made by the same Creator and bring Him joy, simply by being. There's no requirement for them to be more than what they are; He was satisfied the moment He made them. Playing music is a definitely a privilege, but more important than any song or experience are people and relationships. We are uniquely individual and wonderfully different from any other, yet we are the same body. The music we make together is the real pleasure and praise to our God. Unity transcends the voice of one.

As you evaluate your place in the band or on a team, I want to invite you to give yourself a break from the pressure to prove anything to anyone. You can do your best and no more. What people do with it and how they respond is their deal and responsibility. You answer to God for you and you alone. Remember: "The mind set on the Spirit is life and peace" (Rom. 8:6).

For worship that God can inhabit, there must be unity. We could use less style and great performances and more unified, concerted worship. It's a good thing to step back and look at what we're doing and calling worship. If we forge ahead with our agendas and plans at the expense of relationships, we do ourselves more harm than good, and it's a hindrance to spirit and truth. God is always interested in your heart, but also the others in your band. The more your hearts are in sync, the better your music sounds, and the more room there is for Him to inhabit your praise.

This I confess comes from my own personal struggle; I have to work hard to overcome my issues and be at peace. Though I'm laid back in most people's eyes, truth is I'm wound tighter than a golf ball sometimes, so I repent and pray a lot. I do, however, enjoy more freedom now than ever before. I can say this at least: I will die a very happy man for all the incredible moments of joy I've had playing music with friends.

4

The Creative Band

To all the creators who would write songs for the body of Christ, I hereby free you from the temptress of mediocrity, I hereby release you from the captivity of form, and I compel you into the unknown and beautiful wilderness of authentic creativity to find your unique voice in such a way as to give voice to those who need to sing their joys or sorrows for the redemptive purposes and joy of God.

—Casey McGinty, Senior Vice President, EMI CMG Publishing

Authenticity

There are approximately 250 thousand people gathered here in Lagos, worshipping God in one huge loud voice. It's an amazing and very significant event for Nigeria, as they celebrate 50 years of independence and reclaim their country for Christ.

A host of talents have come to lead in worship and prayer. Don Moen, who I am here with, was appropriately called the Patriarch of Worship and Gospel Music of Africa by one of the key leaders in Nigeria. He was blazing the trail in worship long before it was the movement we've come to know, and the Africans regard him as a pioneer and father in the faith. Around the globe, people know every word to his songs, a testimony to the impact of his ministry.

Don has lived a unique life as worship leader, musician, songwriter, minister, and record company president, truly an exceptionally gifted human being. I've grown to admire and love him as I travel the world with him, and consider him a great ambassador of Christ to the Nations. I ask him this morning as we leave Nigeria to inspire me with a word for bands, and here's what he says: "Authenticity!" Coming from a record company president that would say enough, but it says even more from a man chasing after the heart of God and His kingdom.

Though it's normal to grow up taking in the world around us—with it becoming a part of us and shaping us along the way—as believers in Christ, we are to model our lives after a whole other kingdom than the one we know here. One way we do that is by living and being who we are made to be: the authentic and real you and me.

If you are a band in pursuit of common goals together, you no doubt understand something about the process of finding your vibe, your sound, your look, your edge, your identity, and so on. It's part of the deal. But more important than any sound you make, of course, is the life you live, which speaks volumes over your tone. In my experience, it's not so much the sound that's hard to find; it's maturity and understanding of how to live with a kingdom perspective. Without a vision of who and what we're called to be, we wander aimlessly, following others' ideas and perceptions. The vision can't just be to be known, or have successful songs in the Church or marketplace; we have greater responsibility than that alone.

Silly as it may seem, it is normal practice for companies to bring in coaches to help artists know what to say from the stage or in an interview. I'll be honest: if we don't have a clear idea of what our passion is and an understanding of truth enough to communicate it, then no one else can give it to us. For it to be authentic, it must come from the treasures of our own hearts and communion with God Almighty. Otherwise we're just borrowing a medium or platform to exploit ourselves.

Being authentic is a unique balance of seeking first the Kingdom of God while stewarding talents and spiritual gifts. We can certainly make it more complicated than it needs to be, and for the most part, it's not rocket science. Music and relationships grow naturally in the collective mix of a band. Where authenticity really comes into play is deciding together what you're going to pursue and chase after. It's about the choices we make.

Here are just some of the questions we need answers for. Will we allow others to dictate or define our vision and calling? Do we need to be well known to do our ministry? Do we desire most what others have or what God desires for us? Are we following or leading? Do we want to minister or entertain?

We don't pass judgment on anyone else's life; we are responsible to God alone for what we do with what we have. But we can sharpen and challenge one another to remember what the main thing is. I've not met many driven, creative types that didn't want to know how to get out there in front of people or achieve at least some success— worship leaders included. Again, I think that is a natural part of our humanity, but our choices do reflect our passion.

My challenge with regard to Don's word for the day, *authenticity*, is this:

- Set your sights on giving back to God the most real, honest, creative, and genuine expressions from your hearts, before looking at the world or marketplace to determine what's vibey, cool, and marketable.

- Be more committed to setting the right example as a believer than you are willing to do whatever it takes to be promoted.

- Define and focus *now* on the vision and ministry God gives you, more than on pursuing companies and deals to help you with future ministry plans—they'll find you!

- Don't be found void of what to say or confused about the truth of the gospel of Jesus, which is central to faith and worship.

If you will aim for the Kingdom first, I truly believe that God will put you in great places of influence, big and small. Most bands can play, but not all can lead by example; which will you be?

An Original

After listening to a CD, which was very good but a bit more than a hat-tip to about three different bands I grew up listening to, I had a conversation about what makes a band or artist original. The music on the CD went beyond being influenced by to copying. My thought was: I'd rather just listen to the originals. It's hard to be original, but I believe we should be, because I feel that as Christians, we should lead, not follow, in all we do. Being the best you makes total sense to me. When we use the tools in our skill set and give our best to God, what comes out may reflect some of what we're influenced by but should above all be real and true—an innate and passionate response to the Creator.

As it relates to worship, I think we rob God, others, and ourselves when we reduce creativity to only that, which we do in the assembly. Whatever we create should reflect the heart of a worshipper. Throughout history, artists from the Church have impacted both the Church and outside culture. The key ingredient is always God's presence in and on it, whatever *it* is. When God chooses to anoint something, it works in all spheres. Shouldn't the focus then be on finding and doing what God blesses? Thankfully it's not limited to only a few, but all that set themselves apart for The Lord can be used.

My hope is to inspire you as a band to aim high, whether you serve by leading your congregation in worship or have a passion to just play what God has put within you. Do what you do with a glad heart, as excellently and uniquely as only *you* can.

While at the NAMM show two weeks ago in Anaheim, CA, I was hit by how big a tribe we really are. It's one of the largest industry trade shows in the world. It helped to see again how vast creativity really is. God is, to say the least, creative. It's like being in the biggest paint store in the world for an artist. There were more colors than one could ever use, but certainly a few to add to the palette. Eventually I had to just focus on finding the ones that would help me do what I do better, because I found myself wandering around overwhelmed. The unbelievable number of incredibly talented people alone was overwhelming. Most artists short-circuit a bit when they encounter others more talented than themselves; it does something to you. The desire to be noticed or deemed worthy is insatiable and all consuming. It leads to a dead end and makes for a life full of insecurity. We're not called to be famous but to serve, which is a humble state to exist in and flies in the face of the self-consumed nature and lifestyle of most artists. Doesn't mean that God won't make some famous; King David was pretty well known.

Are you ever overwhelmed by all the stuff around you or intimidated by others being used, noticed, or rewarded more? Does it make you feel less significant or that you don't count as much? Your security in Christ ultimately determines how original you are. If who you are isn't good enough for you, then you'll be miserable. We tend to judge ourselves based on accolades or others' responses to us, especially our creative offerings. We do this even in worship. But who can really judge what God feels about the sacrifice of another? When you offer the best you, that's all He's asked you to do. It's not received on the basis of your merit or good, but Jesus's sacrifice and goodness.

This truth will liberate driven, passionate, creative types, if you let it. It really doesn't matter how hip or marketable you are. Be of substance more than style. Find the colors, sounds, and textures that make you, you. Originality is not as much about sound and look as it is being salt and light, in a very dark world around us. It's caring more for the others wandering around overwhelmed and lost. Who've yet to discover the awesome truth: that they're loved just as they are by a merciful God in Heaven.

No matter how good the artists are that I appreciate and respect in the world, whose gifts and talents were given to them by the same God that gave me mine, what I aspire to be most is not as good as or better than them, but who God made me to be, an original.

Songwriting as a Band

Songs are the heart of a band. Whether you are a worship-leading band or otherwise, it's helpful to understand what makes a song strong. I am asked a lot about the process of writing, so I've put some basic thoughts down that will hopefully help you craft better songs.

Foundations first!

- *Creativity* is from and for God, a talent we are responsible to steward and a reflection of our passion. What makes the ultimate difference is God's presence and blessing on it; make that the goal.

- *Integrity*: All that we do should be holy. David sang and expressed his heart using his own words, drawing from his life experiences, good and bad, and God judged his to be a heart after His own. Be pure and honest, and live a lifestyle of worship. Please God, and let Him define your creative expression.

- *Reality*: If you aim to contend with, and be relevant to, pop culture and industry, there are costs to count. Ignorance is no excuse for our own irresponsibility. Become educated, know why you do what you do, and don't be compromising. Notoriety won't give you a ministry. Unguarded ambition leads to a self-consumed drive for success, in the name of God. Allow Him to promote you. Whatever comes from your heart to God is valid but may not be for anyone but you.

- *Focus*: The best writers and artists are focused. Whatever your level of talent and proficiency, you can invest time to become the best you. It is not by happenstance: the more you do it, the better you become.

Songwriting 101, The Big Four:

1.   Melody = singability
2.   Lyric = truth, honesty, emotion, passion, and integrity

3. Hook = memorability (the lyrical hook is sometimes in the song title)
4. Form = road map and structure

Note: There are no absolute formulas or rules. They've all been broken, proving that people connect to and like what they will. The strongest songs use "The Big Four" as tools to render a work unique to the writer. The best ones have proven over time to be the ones that connect the most with others and have the most originality.

The Process:

1. Start with what is most natural: music, melody, or lyric.
2. Develop ideas and put into a form—e.g., VCVCBC or VVCVCC.
3. Establish a lyric and melodic hook that sells and delivers the title.
4. Document it while it's fresh.
5. Collaborate, especially if you're weaker in a particular area.

Tips: Economize your words, edit continuously, step away, and revisit—helps discover what pops or sticks. Be open to and seek constructive criticism from those better than you; take it in, apply what you can, choose not to be offended by it.

The Mechanics:

1. *Demo*: First, create a work version using what you have to capture the song in the original form. For a more produced version (demo), record the song using the highest quality standard you can, so that it's presentable and pitchable. When pitching songs, remember: you're competing against demos that sound like records already. The better the demo is, the more it helps, but don't mortgage the farm and demo beyond your means! Being diligent to organize, catalog, and document your songs will only always help you.

2. *Arranging*: The arrangement helps deliver a song both live and recorded. It never hurts to economize timewise; cut out long intros and turnarounds, especially if you plan to pitch your songs. Most recorded projects start with good songs, then a good arrangement. The goal is to make it relevant and creative to suit the need—e.g., arranging for worship more involves flow, dynamics, and key; arranging for a recording involves more consideration for form, length, and style. The key is relative more for the artist/singer than a congregation.

3. *Production*: Production is the process for recording songs. It can be as complex and expensive as you choose. Good producers bring out the best in songs and artists; assemble the right team for the job. Good production can make or break a song or an artist. Capture the most relevant and viable form of the song, in order to deliver it to a specific audience. It is a good tool for developing artistry and excellence, while forcing you to hone in on a better, more finished version of your material.

4. *Publishing*: Because songs have earning potential, it's an issue of stewardship, hence publishing. Royalties are monies collected by organizations such as ASCAP or BMI and referred to as "mechanicals." They are split 50/50 between writer and publisher according to a statutory rate of approximately $0.09 per song, per unit sold or manufactured. Until you've signed publishing over to someone else, *you're the publisher*. First, decide if the business of publishing is one you even need to be in, and learn how it works. The role of a publisher is to develop, expose, and administrate songs. The main concern really is protecting your songs by copywriting them with the Library of Congress. If you already have songs circulating, then you need some type of publishing administration at work on your behalf. Your choices are: sign to a major publisher that does administration, or procure an independent copyright administration firm for a percentage/fee. Should you decide, you can also start your own publishing company fairly easily. For more information, contact ASCAP, BMI, or SESAC, which are the top three Performance Royalty Organizations or PROs.

   Note: When sending songs to publishers, send two or three, not ten. Send to someone's attention preferably, and include lyrics and contact info. Slick press packs cost money and normally end up in the trash. In reality, they're not looking too far outside their own sphere for songs, and unless sent via referral or personal relationship, they likely won't be heard. By all means be diligent, but understand, very few songs arrive on the scene this way, though there are some exceptions.

Dynamics

Everybody in at the top and we'll meet up at the end! That's what it feels like sometimes; we count in a song, everyone plays from beginning to end, and first one there's the winner. That's why we're here right, to play? Yes, but music is much more musical when it's dynamic—ebbing, flowing, moving, and breathing.

In my high school jazz band, more than once my director had to call me out in front of the whole band to say things like, "Too loud," "Too busy," "Listen more," "Play less," or "Stick to the music till you know it better." He'd also been in a band with the guitar player of one of my favorite rock bands in the day, which meant I did respect him, even if he got on to me. He would often encourage me with things like, "If you wanna do what he [the guitar player I loved] does," (and I did—bad) "then you need to become more disciplined and pay attention, because he's no idiot. He knows more than four chords and how to noodle a bit." I wasn't the only one he said those things to, but I took them with me for sure and have remembered them. He helped me grow up as a player and band member. That season marked the beginning of my becoming a more dynamic and tasteful player.

Regarding dynamics, at some point as we mature, we should ideally be able to contribute to the big picture of a song, not simply play it without too many errors or just to get to the end on time. A couple of things helped me put it in better perspective. For one, being in Blues Counsel, a band with three guitar players and a keyboard player. It's a recipe for a mess if you don't listen to what the others are doing and learn to complement. Two, listening to the way two different engineers mix the same song. One may mute that part you spent all night crafting in a particular spot, while the other features or highlights it. You may realize that when it was taken away, the song breathed more. Many times they'll peel things back, strip it down, and simplify; then, as the song goes along, add them back gradually or sparingly. All of the sudden, a song has a different life. Everything changes in the dynamics of a mix.

Live, it's the same. It can sound like one solid wall of stuff coming at you all at once, which is very linear and pointed. Or it can unfold like a story with peaks and valleys. The difference can mean inviting listeners into the journey by taking them along, or demanding they hear it forcibly, whether they want to or not. These kinds of dynamics have been used to manipulate and affect emotions throughout history, both for good and bad. Sheer volume alone affects how and what we hear. There are many colors in a song and power in music; God made it just that way.

Dynamics in worship are important then, as they help us move with or against God's Spirit, who is always leading us somewhere. Sometimes the routine of playing songs the same way over and over can become a hindrance more than help. No day is the same. In every gathering, needs are different. So we need flexibility and sensitivity as leaders and players in order to respond accordingly.

In all the bands I've been part of, members were invited to join because they each brought something to the table. When I put a band together now to lead worship, I do think a lot about how the person reacts and flows in worship, as well as his or her heart. I don't want to drag a band along musically if I don't have to but rather move together with them in sync, for the purpose of entering into worship and helping others do likewise. I also would like for it to sound good. I'm not a snob about it, but I do know when it sounds bad. So I work to make it as good as possible. That doesn't mean that I won't incorporate younger or less experienced players and singers either, which is just as important, and there are ways to do it effectively.

Not that it's wrong, but some worship programs run on the basis that everyone who wants to join can. Or they'll put as many as can fit on the stage up there. Both can spell disaster or misery musically speaking, if it's done arbitrarily without thinking about what each member contributes dynamically. Before you're offended, I'm not suggesting that music is more important than heart. It's not. But I will say this: we give more thought to the food we order sometimes than we do to working towards excellence in worship. We wouldn't throw a palette of paint on a canvas and expect the colors to miraculously morph into a thing of beauty—unless it's abstract, I guess, and to some that's beautiful. Still, it takes work and *some level of talent*, right?

Every ministry has to determine their criteria for involving people, and I respect the many ways it's done. We devote a lot of time, and rightly so, to being right theologically, spiritually, and so forth. My point is, very simply, we do have the capability, technology, talent, and opportunity, so we should do our best—to give God the best we can.

So Jam Then

There's a feeling I love that happens occasionally during a sound check. You've got your sounds dialed in, you're up and running, and the band starts in on a groove or a jam. Next thing you know, it comes to life, maybe a cool song idea, and then someone interrupts, busts the groove—bringing the cool little moment to a screeching halt and reminding us what we're there to do. It's a major bummer, but you have to stop because you know they're right! Great things can happen spontaneously when there's room for it.

There's much to be said about spontaneity and creativity in worship. I wonder if we allow it enough, honestly. If you grew up jamming a lot, then you know how fulfilling, productive, and fun it is. You get to spread your wings and fly a little, with no one to reel you back in just when you're starting to take off and really enjoy it. It's part of discovering who God made you as a musician and worshipper. But for most, it's a foreign thought that we'd bring that part of ourselves into a worship service. It actually scares some. I do believe we need to reclaim some of the *spontaneity* in our worship, and it shouldn't scare us to death or be so foreign. But I also believe there needs to be order, or Paul wouldn't have addressed it so pointedly.

When David danced naked and took off down the street in rather wildly abandoned praise, I doubt it was all that nice and tidy. Nor prepared, but God loved it! *My gut says that if you tried that today you'd be locked up, so you be the judge of what to do with his example.* I do feel some of that spirit in me (except for the dance naked part) and see it in other players too: an inner beckoning to be released and let go. But there seems to be little or no permission to do it.

Years ago I remember watching a little girl dance at my Church. That wasn't something I grew up with in Church, so it's always been a struggle for me to get it, let alone do it. But I watched her and secretly wished that I could be that free. Not to do it every Sunday in Church necessarily, but so I could experience the feeling of not caring and being oblivious to what others around me think. But I always have cared too much, and with good reason; the list was a mile long of what not to do in Church, and dancing was on it. I still ask God for that kind of freedom, and my wife is awaiting the day I break into a dance, stunning everyone, me included. Who knows, God is big, right?

I'll walk outside the lines here a bit and hope you'll read on. For the record, I'm somewhere between a recovering United Metho-Baptist and Charis-Moderate. Time and space aren't comfortable for most leaders in a worship setting and can be equally boring for those in the pews. I think we ultimately fear what we can't control. I also know that it can swing way far out there, which brings up a whole other set of issues we don't like to deal with. So in general, we just avoid it and stick with what we've come to know and trust works on either side of the extremes. Not to say we should aim for a particular feeling or emotion in worship every time; it's not about that either. But is what we know and are comfortable with all there is?

Most of us would say we want whatever God has, but it's still a challenge to *let* Him into our program sometimes. We have to be brave enough to ask for it and pliable enough to move over when it happens—without controlling the life right out of it because it takes longer than what time we've allotted. There has to be room, and that's the hard part. So we aim and ask for whatever God wants it to look and be like. None of my personal experiences are enough to suggest to you as something to attain to. What matters more is learning to experience His joy and freedom as the unique congregation you are.

My goal has become to enjoy and walk away from worship times knowing I've given my whole heart, and adequate time, to God. Because He's worth it and deserves it! I'm learning still, every day, to live my freedom without expecting a good response from anyone but God. I also feel no need to impose my freedom on another's context when uninvited, because it's just rude. Whom The Son sets free is free indeed, and that also applies to worship. What I do have cannot be taken from me by anyone, even if they disagree with or don't get it. Yet I can control whether to impose my freedom on others or not. For any number of reasons, some feel they must impose their personal freedom, as if to prove something, but it's normally distracting and brings the person more attention than the actual freedom. This kind of behavior, and even abuse, are the very reasons many are scared to allow more freedom, unfortunately.

There is more, but it won't just appear out of thin air. We have to need and want it first for ourselves. It can't be about what is or is not happening in our particular Church worship service. We don't have to chase it around the world to find it either. God will move right here and now, in time and space, to give us what He already made provision for on His cross: freedom! Once we have it in our heart, it will permeate our playing, our whole being ultimately, and spark a revival of one that is contagious.

Here is a step you can take toward finding your freedom, borrowed from an old friend and hero of mine, Don Potter. Learn to play to the wall. In your own private space, face a wall, then play and sing your heart out to God. It's hard to be distracted by others there. You will likely exhaust your repertoire faster than you'd think and be amazed how hard it is to stay beyond 20 to 30 minutes. If you keep at it long enough, you will go beyond the songs you know to new melodies, prayers, and so forth. The more you do it, the more you zero in on God and away from distraction and self. This exercise helps take the focus and dependence off of those around you in corporate settings. It's about *you* alone with The Lord, using your talent to express *your* heart to Him.

Another way to move toward a more free worship time is to create a context aside from your main worship service, where you and a few others come together and just play to God.

More people provide a greater sense of security to find freedom in worship—it's a bigger wall! God isn't scared of us testing our wings in worship—a larger group is a safer way to do that. The idea is that we are learning to respond to Him, not impress Him. The more we respond to Him, the better we then lead others in worship. Here again God sees your heart; do it for Him.

As a band, you can easily set time aside where there's nothing required of you. It's just your offering to God, so you can let go, kind of like we did as kids—just jamming. So jam then! Here's your permission slip—the Psalms are full of more examples in case you're a skeptic.

The Fifth Wheel

I've had the opportunity to work with many soundmen/audio engineers over the years, and I learned early to make good friends with them, as they can easily turn you down and make life unpleasant for the band. On the flip side, the band can make an engineer equally as miserable. Need I say, everything is better when everyone's happy?

Sir George Martin, often referred to as the fifth Beatle, played a key role in capturing their talent and passion; he was truly one of the team. A band can't go far without interfacing with live sound reinforcement systems and technicians. But who starts out by asking a soundman to be in the band? They're often like fifth wheels and aren't considered when they should be! However, the good ones are highly valued by those who know their worth on the team and become indispensable.

I happen to be sitting with just such a guy, Chuck Harris, on a flight from Bali to Singapore. He's traveled the world with some greats; some of them won't leave home without him. Plus he knows some stuff, so I picked his brain for all our benefits. I asked Chuck what he would say to a band and for a few key things that it would help players and singers onstage to know. Here are "Chuckie's Tips"!

Pay attention to:

1. *Tone!* A band's tone is the soundman's secret weapon. A good tone is hard to mess up, *though it can be done*! If each player works hard on his or her own tone, it helps me immensely.

2. *Arrangements:* Make sure everything has its own sonic place. Don't be too busy.

3. *Stage Volume:* The more seasoned the player, the less tone is an issue. It seems they get great tone with less volume on stage, which gives me greater freedom overall.

4. *Microphone Placement and Proximity:* Find the sweet spot, and don't drift from it. Be more conscientious; it's part of your instrument ultimately.

5. *Focus!* Don't make me have to work to get your attention or flag you down while we're getting sounds. Stay focused and organized while we're dialing everyone in, and it goes so much faster.

6. *Mix:* Identify what you like and need to hear in your mix. Everyone is different.

7. *In-Ear Monitoring:* Keep both earphones in. When both earphones are in place, they are close to the eardrum, and you can get away with less volume—which is good. With one earphone out, the other ear is flooded with volume as *you turn up*, typically doubling the volume and potentially causing hearing damage.

8. *Silent Stage:* The personal monitor system, such as the Aviom, gives you the ability to dial in and control your own mix, and it keeps the stage volume to a bare minimum, which helps in some environments and again gives more control to the sound operator out front.

The key to doing your best is hearing optimally. Whether you are using wedges or in-ears, it is important to take the time to dial the mix in well—the soundman is your key to doing that. One reason I feel it's good to hear from engineers like Chuck is that they typically understand more about the effects of loud volume, and they have control of the ultimate levels. More than a few musicians and singers I know have suffered long-term hearing loss from abuse of volume.

So take your sound techs to Starbucks, get to know them, and let them help you. Treat them as members of the band; they're your key to sounding better!

Worship Is Visual

Our culture is fixated on and enamored with appearances. Even if we think we don't care much about what others think, we kind of do really, right? Just watch commercials; not by accident are there images associated with most every product. We are visual people, and what we see can influence even our wallets.

Though we don't often hear sermons on how we look onstage, especially in a positive light, the subject has relevance. You can be sure that you'll get an email as soon as you do something that rubs someone the wrong way on Sunday, especially the right someone. There are always those prone to complain. We'd go nuts trying to please them all—we simply can't. Most would agree that worship is about the heart and lifestyle, not the wardrobe. That's not what I'm referring to here either. Others do notice our expression and countenance, and it matters—that's what I want to address.

David's appearance and expression earned him praise, scorn, favor, blessing, and influence. It was said of Joseph by people who counted that The Lord was with him and gave him success in everything he did. Fruit is something you can see with your eyes. The Word says we will know a tree by the fruit it bears. It also says that from the abundance of the heart, the mouth speaks. So what's inside does come out and is obvious to others.

In two cases recently, both involving drummers, numerous people commented how they particularly noticed them and were impacted just watching them play and worship. Their smiles, their joy, their passion—all made a difference. Any number of players could've executed the music just as well (maybe), but it wasn't about that. There was more to it than the playing. There are some very impressive players and talents in the world, but what usually confounds others is not the skill, though it happens, but the attitudes, responses, expressions, personalities, and so on. We know whether someone is genuinely humble or not, full of themselves, insecure, or whatever. We've all seen the most unlikely have greater impact than the most gifted, over and over. And also some of the most beautiful and amazing talents, completely yielded to God, and therefore used mightily. A common denominator is, like Joseph, knowing where it comes from and whom the credit belongs to. That spills over into our countenance naturally, making it hard to fake what's really underneath the surface. Psalm 40:3 says: "He put a new song in my mouth, a hymn of praise to our God. *Many will see and fear The Lord and put their trust in him.*"

There's a difference between judging and criticizing what we see on the worship platform, and noticing and sensing it. It's sad how critical Christians can be of our own, when we have no right to be and are warned not to in the Bible. But we are human, and so we do it sometimes. It's not bad or wrong that we are aware of or stimulated by what we see and experience. While we don't lead in order to be noticed, we are noticed because we are up front leading.

The presence of God within us is naturally visible as we play, sing, and lead. For some it's hard to separate ourselves from a *style we've learned*. Being free, emotional, and passionate is wonderful—we need more of it. It's when we, in that freedom, demonstrate total disregard for those we are worshipping alongside and leading that we become selfish and distracting to others. An example would be how two leaders can lead the same song with completely different outcomes and experiences—one evoking elation and the other agitation—simply because of the delivery style. When we attempt to manipulate feelings or generate particular responses by using a certain style, that's when it's wrong, I think. If the style is just part of who we are, and we're not attempting to do anything other than lead and worship genuinely, then it's really other people's issues to let it hinder them from entering in themselves.

My encouragement is not that we go get in front of a mirror to practice facial expressions and our favorite "holy" moves (although if you decide to do that, please record and post it on YouTube for the rest of us to enjoy) but that we take notice of our own inner condition and what we consciously or subconsciously convey to others during worship. Ultimately, we want others to see and fear The Lord. Are we reflecting His countenance and joy—in spite of trouble, pain, or circumstances? Joseph obviously had something great going on inside. Prosperity and favor didn't mean all was well. He was still a slave, hated by his brothers, and locked inside a dungeon, yet the powers that be always recognized His God was with him. That's an example worth noting and following. Hard, but worth it to develop his kind of keeping power and resolve to trust in God instead of his own emotion and feeling.

David also demonstrated that whether we're ticked off, sad, and angry; or happy, joyful, and excited, it's okay to come as we are. We don't ever fool God, and He deals with us as a loving father, not a dictator. So let's be real and honest, but also mindful that how we appear and what others see does make a difference.

People are not always watching intentionally; sometimes it's expectantly or even desperately—wanting and needing God to touch them. We cannot control those who look on and judge, whether or not it was a good worship performance. But it is healthy to be aware of what we are portraying, so as to align with the Holy Spirit. We can only play, lead, and worship our best, as unto God. In the process, we may well be used as conduits of Jesus's love and mercy.

5

Mentoring

Being a mentor makes a Godly deposit in others that will shape their lives for Christ and multiply itself throughout generations. Love God, gain influence in people's lives, and freely give what you have learned in order to help them live for Christ and do the same in the hearts of others.

—Rick Cua

Incite and Inspire

There are a few older musician friends that have had real impact on me and helped shape who I've become. What they all had in common was an ability to share the stage, make room, encourage and challenge me at crucial times in my life and development.

In the coming years, our vision for worship teams and bands needs to broaden. It has to incorporate helping the next-generation leaders. In historic human fashion, we've come to revere the current modern sound and style of worship music. This isn't all bad. Historically, we learn that God is always leading us onward and has often gone around those associated with the last move in order to usher in the next one. Usually because we can't see beyond the tradition we know, love, and protect.

What we do now is largely about leading songs in corporate gatherings that the congregation can sing along with. While that's certainly important, evangelism is also part of the worship equation. Some are called to go beyond the walls of Churches to lead worship in a way that may offend our modern worship-culture mindset. If we only support and encourage the congregationally friendly model of worship leading, we may lose the ones behind us who God has gifted to win their generation of lost peers to Christ.

Here's why I bring it up. I can't count the times I've heard this story from leaders all over. "We started this thing, where we let the young musicians and youth come to just play their music, gave them a room to do it, and it grew. But it seemed to have no real direction or leadership, and the music wasn't really worshipful. So we felt we needed to shut it down." *And so they shut it down!* I actually know of one Church that had a thriving worship gathering for young people that met just below the old sanctuary where the traditional service was going on at the same time. Guess who won that battle? They nixed (killed) the contemporary, noisy service, and now they just don't have a contemporary one. And then they wonder where all the young people have gone. I know it's a dilemma, and I even understand it to a degree, but it's still sad that this battle frequently stirs division instead of breeding opportunity.

Ultimately it's a fear of the unknown and inability to control something or fit it into our box that shuts it down, but it shouldn't. Not meaning to offend, but I lovingly say we must get over it and figure out how not to drive the future leaders of the Church away! Employ all means to bring them in. It will be messy, look different, sound different, but it's a process to lead them into maturity in The Lord—and that's what discipleship is about.

So my challenge is: *incite and inspire* the next generation's bands, which may well be on the frontlines of a Jesus revolution in the near future. There are many opinions and philosophies, but I think it's much simpler than we make it. Right where you are, with what you have, you can do something to play a role in helping them.

Here's how it clicked for me. Bryan was 14 when I first heard him play bass, and he was already good! By the time he turned 16, he was really good, and I don't think I'd ever known a kid so given to The Lord and such a pure-hearted worshipper at his age. I was leading worship for a lot of youth events then and was encouraged by my wife to ask Bryan and another "kid" named Miles—also 16—to join me. At first it scared me. I had no idea what it'd sound like but I did it, and for two years or so, they came along. The short story is, Bryan went on to work alongside some renowned worship leaders and continues to be a great leader and shining example. He and his music have a voice that his peers relate to more than they ever would to mine. It thrills and excites me to even be around him and to have been a small part of his story. Seeing God pour out opportunities and blessings on him is awesome. There was a day when I would have been jealous of that; now I honestly delight in it. Bryan and I share a great relationship still; in truth he's impacted my life more than

I have his, affecting how and why I do what I do. Miles also went on to do some incredible things—I wish I had time to tell his story too.

If we can prioritize people and help them in small ways to do what they do, we will earn a place of influence in their lives. It's that simple! If you have to find a barn just to let the youth of your Church crank it to 11 and go for it—do it. Befriend them, hang out, *and wear earplugs if you need to.* Defend their space from the critics and antagonists, and pray for wisdom to lead and mentor them in a Godly way. Join the generations, be a bridge builder. By taking young musicians and bands under your wing, you could be preparing the next Beatles or U2 to lead a generation to the only true hope and answer, Jesus.

To all the youth, I want to remind you of Paul's words to Timothy: "Don't let anyone look down on you because you are young, but set an example for the believers in speech, in life, in love, in faith and purity" (1 Tim. 4:12). Go do what God has put in your heart!

From Within

We used to live a world where hymns and choruses were all we had and deemed acceptable for use in worship services. But for the past 15-plus years, we've seen an influx of songs, as God once again turned the heart of His people back to himself. Now there are more songs than ever, and most Churches have the top CCLI list in constant rotation. All that's a good thing, and it's amazing how God has used some of these songs and the leaders who've written them.

One thing I'm personally passionate about is seeing the indigenous expression of people groups arise from their own creative communities. It is powerful to travel around the world and join with others to sing the same song in many languages. It used to be that no matter where I went, 90 to 99 percent of the songs we sang were from the West and had been translated. Hardly ever would I hear a worship song written from within a foreign culture. As I'd get to know the musicians, I'd find out they had volumes of music of their own, but little of it was ever used in their Churches. So a long time ago, I started asking why.

There's always been a bit of a rub between musicians and the Church. A brief look into history paints the picture of an ongoing struggle for artists and musicians in the Church family to find their place or voice. So it's nothing new. I hear the discontent from both sides: the artists/worship leaders and the leadership that are looking out for their people. Both are scared to push the envelope too far for many different reasons. I can't cover all of the reasons here but would like to talk about what we can do to encourage the new, unique, and fresh creativity that should be flowing from the ground up in the Church. And being that we're a diversely gifted group, *thankfully* it's going to look different from one body to the next.

This leads me to another question: Why do we primarily look outside our own Church first? I understand that not every Church has a songwriter or worship leader in the midst, and by all means we use what we have available, but we should also be looking for and cultivating writers and leaders from within, constantly mining for them, even if it takes years to see results. We tend to be importers more than exporters, yet every Church has something to give away. Again, I get it. But does it have to stay that way? Some have long been determined to change their ways and are doing a wonderful job. Others are still in the infancy stage. But hopefully, we can agree on the need for each Church to begin to organically inspire and cultivate music ministers.

Some things we can do, if we are willing to make some room, are:

1. *Plant some seeds.* It starts young, needless to say. Begin by making an investment now into your future leaders and artists. Buy a sound system, and donate a room where they can make some noise. Try not to attach a bunch of strings either, let them run free a bit. The point at this stage is not really to have them replicate what our older folks are doing upstairs or over in the posh sanctuary. In the next 10 years, trends are going shift again, and we may not recognize much of what is now our normal. That's okay! Many well-known bands and artists have come from the Church. Unfortunately though, not many stay in the Church. Some of that has to do with our own inability to allow and provide an environment of true friendship for them to grow up in. We need to embrace the apprentice mentality. Lead and instruct without tying their hands behind their backs, prohibiting them from being uniquely themselves.

2. *Venture out.* In addition to learning the Top 20 CCLI, begin to prioritize the incorporation of new songs from your own people. To do that, you may need to educate both your writers and your people. For sure we need to become less critical and people pleasing in worship. Of all places, there should be a safe and welcoming atmosphere in the Church to receive what's coming from one of our own family members—instead of an immediate judgment of its worth in comparison to our favorite worship song or leader.

It will be clumsy and not always good, but are we at least making room to try it? See it as tapping a well; in time, if you keep priming the pump, you'll have water flowing from your own cistern. What a concept!

3. *Build community and friendship, locally and regionally.* When we pool our resources and band together, the impact is deeper and wider. Though we normally want to see it as our own thing, in truth we're only a part of the Church in our cities; no one of us has or owns the domain for Church. Think about starting a local or regional gathering on a regular basis to encourage and inspire one another. Pray and worship beyond your differences, and ask God to be at work within your own area through your creative community. Great things have started that way, and we all share the benefits.

More than ever, the world needs to see a band of united Christians, loving and embracing our own, well. Unfortunately the road is littered with too many that have witnessed the opposite of unity and run the other way. Sadly, some of those are of the most creatively gifted the world's ever known.

The work starts at home for it to come from within. We can only give away what we have, so let's get busy!

Managing Teams

Musicians are notorious for not being good managers. Wanna get one to turn down? Put a chart in front of them. Wanna drive one crazy? Give them a noncreative responsibility or project to manage. At least for me, it requires a whole lot of effort to do the administrative things. I glaze over and feel the cloud roll in the second my groove is busted or I have to switch sides of my brain. Relate?

If you've ever seen a *Where Are They Now* documentary on your favorite band, you know they most likely broke up due to some relational, nightmarish conflict they were unable to resolve in a mature manner. *At least until decades later when the money ran out and someone dreamed up a reunion tour or album!* In most bands, there are diverse talents and serious quirks in the mix—and the more creative, the messier too. The movie *That Thing You Do* was a great peak into the reality show that most bands are. So imagine then: you take the musician dynamics, insert them into a worship experience with the added Church dynamics, and it's a whole other world.

Once God apprehends and bridles the heart and its passion, there's no end to where He can take it. The Church is the stream by which God's love flows to the world. As a family, if we can stay together through all the hurt feelings, failed expectations, betrayals, and the like, then the light and truth of Jesus's redeeming love and power will be the testimony God uses to reach the world. This should be the objective of every band/team that professes to worship Jesus and wants to lead others to Him.

For Christians, it has to start with what our God values most: relationship and communion. What makes a team work well is good management but, more importantly, good relationships. From the school of "How Not to Do It" comes the following insight. I hope it helps.

1. *Relationships—tend them, don't use and abuse them.* It's easy to spot talent and normal to want to include someone on a team. Not so easy to keep your motives selfless versus selfish. We really do need to care more for the person than the talent or objective. Doing so earns us the opportunity to speak into and influence others versus bossing them around. True, it is the responsibility of leadership to carry out the vision, and not everything is democratic. Still others will only admire your talent and/or position for so long. If you use them and/or wear them out, they'll just say no in the future, and that's their prerogative.

    Ask yourself: Why do I want them on the team, and does it mean them becoming someone other than who they are?

2. *Responsibility—a constant balance of duty and priority.* Managers dole out responsibilities and are required to get the job done. However, what's different about most worship teams is that they're normally volunteers. Managing them requires even more flexibility. I don't think the worship team should be anyone's highest priority in life, especially over family relationships and other God-given responsibilities. Amazingly, some treat it as a position appointed by the President. I'm not saying it's not important, just that we should only commit having first evaluated all the costs, particularly family. Once we say yes to a job or responsibility, then our yes should mean yes. If the leader or the team member over- or understresses the terms of the commitment, then good, clear communication is required

to keep it from suffering strain that can cause a breakdown. So everyone is responsible for weighing and keeping their commitments, even volunteers.

Ask yourself: is my level of commitment determined by compensation or personal satisfaction?

3. *Outcome—ultimately God's responsibility.* Though we are charged with duties, when it comes to people, we cannot control the outcome. That is very much dependent upon personal choice and free will that are God's gift to all. There are certainly consequences to good and bad choices. The choice not to honor a commitment may mean loss of the opportunity/job/role. The choice to uphold it, go beyond it, and honor it could mean more opportunities in the future. But to attempt to manipulate an outcome creates stress and problems more often than not. I am speaking specifically of worship ministry now. The command is to be holy as He is holy. In worship, the relationship will always be preeminent. We can speak truth, walk in it, do our best in all things, but we cannot do what God reserves the right to do alone: control the outcome. This means we'll all be disappointed sometimes with another's response to our management, choices, or leadership efforts. Best to understand this, give it your best, and learn to chill out. Don't stress over making team members or worship leaders do what you want them to do; you ultimately can't!

Ask yourself: Am I compelled to enforce others' responses or actions in any way?

Good relationships mean healthier teams!

What About the Yoots?

One of the things I do in life and have been doing a very long time is work with youths—or *Yoots*, as I call them. It's a passion for both my wife and me. We run youth events and camps, and lead teams around the world. We are truly inspired by them, and some have become our dearest friends.

What I love about young people is the lack of religious baggage attached to their creative expression. If they've not yet been told "You can't do it that way," then what comes out is naturally free and uninhibited—the way God meant it! Needless to say, the language of music is powerful, despite the fact that the style and relevancy changes from generation to generation. My hope is that we'll embrace this next movement of minstrels and artists and help them lead their generation to Christ. To me, this needs to be a huge focus for anyone who's aiming for a vital, relevant, and thriving worship ministry.

There's a Church down South that I've been going back to for the last eight years, to lead worship for their youth. In that short time, the seven-member youth group has grown to 120-plus in a small community. There were no musicians at first, and now there are bands, singer-songwriters, and worship leaders—a lot of sharp young leaders in general. This happened because the former youth minister, who's a lifelong friend; his pastor; and a group of parents at the Church decided to create time and space for the Yoots to grow their talents and step into their gifting early. They've not just built something for them but allowed them to participate in the building, and now they're a growing force! I've learned a lot from their model, and I've seen it work over and over throughout my friend's youth-ministry career. Though investing in young people is obviously not only about building a team of musicians and artists, the investment made by a youth pastor who's not even a musician, a pastor, and some parents clearly produced a bunch of them. To boot, now one of the former Yoots is the Yoot Director. Now that's how it ought to be!

For starters, we can't be afraid of the messes and issues galore that come along with young, creative people. They're human like us old fogies, and God does not demand they be perfected before they are allowed to step into responsibilities or roles. My buddy is great at spotting talent and giving them a place to use it. I want to challenge those that think you only put the more mature or seemingly together ones up front. I'm not saying make them all elders in your Church, but I am saying let them play a song, run a mixer, play with the lights, operate the multimedia, and so forth. For some, all they need is to feel needed to do anything or be a part of something.

The Church is not so good at letting people *get it* via the Holy Spirit versus our having to tell them what they should be doing and how exactly it should be done. We're all a mess, but God specializes in cleaning up the messy. So invite them all, let them come as they are, that's the Jesus model! Part of the reality is being willing to deal with problems and attitudes, but you can do that without driving them on to someplace else. And that's the reality for us Church: we have a few short years to influence them, or we lose them to a world full of other opportunities. *We have to create opportunities for them.*

Internships are a wonderful thing and a big reason my friends down South have been so fruitful. When people grow in skill level, faith, maturity, and so forth, they carve out a little job description and give those people more responsibility.

If we are willing to be inconvenienced and quick to befriend, we can really help steer the course of young talents. Programs are becoming more of a bore to them; they are drawn to life and friendship. If they feel safe, they'll trust you with the "stuff" in their lives. Artists are already a misunderstood and misfit tribe; it's no wonder they immediately respond to affirmation and praise of any kind. To intentionally deflate them, thinking we're keeping them humble, is a more hurtful way to guide them. If they're a part of a healthy community where they're not high and lifted up but just normal kids, they're more likely to be grounded as they mature. That's in essence the role we play as leaders in the Church. Serving and facilitating doesn't mean accommodating every need; we can't do the impossible, and that's why too many burn out. Mentors guide and steer best, out of true friendship that conveys we're not just the boss but in the battle with them.

I'm going on record to say: I think we are going to see a new breed of worship leader in the near future. It's not enough just to have our own pep rallies and give people what they want to hear every week. The young people I know are already saying that's not what they intend to do. They do want to worship, they do want to serve and be Godly, but they want to be themselves. If history teaches us anything, it's that styles change. What we now know as modern worship won't be modern in a few more years. Not to say songs lose their meaning or impact—many will live on and continue to serve us—but the messengers are going to look and sound different.

There's a boatload of young musicians in our Churches, and just like we did, they're watching their heroes, studying them, and dreaming of how they can do what they do. We have to step up and present them with friendship and encouragement. Church is not an alternative to something else—nor is it a religion. Church should be where people connect with Jesus, the person. Make it inviting!

You Matter

In a world full of stars, it's easy to feel insignificant. We humans love our heroes, and Christian humans are no exception. It's not wrong to appreciate talent, and The Word does say that God gives glory to anyone He chooses. But have you ever felt like what you do up next to what your heroes do is not nearly as important or significant? I think we all have.

With all that we do understand about worship, I believe there's even more we don't. God is vast and immeasurable, always searching the heart and mind, full of understanding, and His ways are not our ways. What pleases Him may be different than what would please us—and it usually is. For this reason, I want to address the hearts of all musicians who have deemed themselves unworthy by comparison to anyone else, ever.

First let me say that what you do is important no matter how small or large it is. You do matter, since your role can be played by no other, only you! There are always better talents, and it is bondage to live in perpetual insecurity over who you're not.

Being a guitar player, I can say this for certain: we are the most aware of, and sensitive to, other players, and we have the biggest egos. We're always scanning the horizon for who's better, considering how we measure up or don't. Living in a town of guitar players like Nashville, where even your waiter may play better than you, it's easy to spot those whose identities are tied to how good or bad they are. Often it's reinforced both positively and negatively by other really good players, who, like kids, can be brutally honest and very competitive.

So if worship is about bringing an offering and sacrifice to The Lord from the heart, which is what God sees, then how sad if we really believe the lie that because we're not as good as some other, we're not as valuable and even beautiful to Him. As you come week by week into worship as a band member, I want to challenge you to do something. Ask God to reveal to you any burdens or expectations you may have that have come from wrong beliefs or clumsy/painful words spoken by others. To worship, in spirit and truth you need only to believe what God says and to be honest with Him about your own heart, period. There's not another measure that ultimately matters. Anyone who passes judgment on your heart is out of order.

Unfortunately there are many abuses of leadership due to misguided, insecure, controlling, and selfish humans. That leads to deep wounds of bitterness and anger, and many other issues that poison the spirit, and it can take years to overcome them. I've known players with great talent and heart to give it up or leave a Church because of another's negative influence. It's a cycle of tragic immaturity and why I think Paul says to the Church, "We need to grow up!"

Here's the truth: if God reveals to you that you don't see yourself the way He does, that you're hindered by criticism of others and negativity of any kind, to give power to it and allow it to rule you is really sin. We give it the authority to control our emotions and our spirit. And it does impede worship in spirit and truth.

Your contribution, if it is given honestly and purely to God, is not only valid, it's all that's expected, and God inhabits your praise. The Blood of Jesus is what sanctifies and makes it holy. So if you find yourself comparing or feeling that you don't count in the bigger picture, think again! Confess that as the lie it is, and don't let the enemy rob you of the joy in worship.

If you are in a situation where leadership is more destructive than edifying, I encourage you to share your frustrations honestly and not let them build up or turn into bitterness that precedes bad behavior on your part. Even if others are in the wrong, you can be free and should live in freedom. The Church cannot continue overlooking abuses in the name of submission and authority. Let's call a spade a spade in love; Paul did. It's not popular and may mean the end of the line for some, but you'll be able to move forward in healthiness and holiness.

There are no real gurus of worship; everyone that we'd put up high is a sinner—redeemed by The Blood of Jesus like us all. They make mistakes, don't always walk in holiness, and are used by the grace of God thankfully. That's good news for me. So be encouraged, give your best, use your noggin, and live free in Christ—as you serve in worship.

6

The Worship Band

Worship leaders should always be asking themselves several questions as they prepare to lead: What is the condition of our own hearts before The Lord as we prepare to lead others in worship? How can we lead others to "hallow" the name of our God? What should the purpose of our worship be? What results are we looking for in the lives of others as we lead them in worship?

—Jim Thomas, Pastor, The Village Chapel, Nashville, Tennessee

Help Your Leader Lead

One of the benefits of playing with the same band a long time is familiarity. The ebb and flow is more natural, because you've evolved together, and each member can predict more instinctively where the others are going. When you have a revolving team, it's not as easy to rely on your second nature. Still, most of us do rely on what we're accustomed to and treat every situation the same. Sometimes people say a band feels more rigid and performance like than worshipful. That can happen when we approach the music like most bands do— playing what we want to play no matter what. This approach dictates how and where the worship service goes, in spite of who's leading.

As a worship leader, one of the hardest things for me is when I know the band is paying no attention to where I am trying to go. Not that it's about me, but it is about leading worship, not simply getting through the songs. If I have the opportunity to rehearse the band, we can work on what I need them to and not to do. But if I don't, quite often I have to settle for the way it is and work within the limitations by changing what I do to fit them. I don't let it hinder me from worshipping or leading, but I may do fewer songs with the band and more alone. I liken it to being driven down the track like a train, not much you can do to stop it once it's barreling on. Some of you know exactly what I mean.

I'll unpack it some just to help give some insight as to what a band can do to hinder a leader without even knowing it. First I'll preface by saying that it's the leader's responsibility to lead and instruct and not just to presume that everyone's there to meet his or her needs. Nor is it a solo venture. If you've invited a band to join you, now it's a team! Also, a pro may sound better the first time, but sounding good isn't always what it's about. The seasoned talent may well miss the point entirely if the goal is simply to execute the song with skill and excellence, with no consideration about how to best support the leader.

Speaking from my perspective and experience only, I have been a support player for many artists and leaders, and I have also been a worship leader most of my life—two different roles completely. When I lead I set the pace. Though I love guitar and it's my instrument, I play it differently when I lead, because more than anything else, I need the team to follow me. To do that best, I usually lead with an acoustic, so I can direct the overall rhythmic and dynamic tone and be the constant for others to zero in and depend on.

Okay, I'm going to pick on everyone in the band equally here, speaking from the worship leader point of view. As a player, *I've also been the culprit at some point, so I'm talking to me too!*

1. The first struggle is typically with the drummer. So we're cruising down the track; during a song, we reach a point where, in spite of the way we may have rehearsed or learned the song, I feel led to back off the intensity dynamically, in order to let the congregation be heard or to wait and pray. You can't always give a cue in the middle of singing and leading, and instead of being cued into to my guitar and watching, the drummer plows on, and now I'm locked into having to go his way instead of where I was intending to go. If I fight back for the tempo, it would just embarrass one or both of us. *It's extremely frustrating,* I will say! I don't mean this critically, but that's a sure sign of a player's level of maturity. The more experienced tend to remain very attuned throughout a song, which frees a leader to lead worship and not just lead the band down the track. Make sense? *Note:* the leader's instrument should be predominant in the drummer's mix. You can still hold the fort down and keep time, but a good drummer also learns to *give time back to the leader* by paying attention!

2. Another struggle, and for sure the most obvious, is with the bass player. Nothing stands out like a sore thumb worse than a wrong note on a bass. It *just hangs there like a hair on a biscuit!* There are three things I deem very important here: play the right notes; play less than you think you should; and right behind that, work with—not against—your drummer. Obvious though it is, bass and drums are the foundation, right? If the two are in sync with me as a leader, I can still drive without the feeling of having to pull everyone along the track. Everything is just better then. Here's another tidbit I've seen employed by some very inexperienced players that makes them actually seem more experienced: if you don't know what you're supposed to play, don't! Play nothing, and we'll all think you're brilliant. Trust me.

3. Next on the list of groove busters is my own tribe, the guitar players. Most noticeable to me is when it comes down dynamically at some point and I'm trying to allow for some space, or even better, transition to another song; rather than lay back and listen to where I may be going, the impulse is to play what I'm playing or add to it. Again, now I'm locked in unless they give me back the space to move. I don't expect the band to be mind readers, but it helps immensely when players listen and complement instead of doing their own thing and hindering, which is what happens a lot. You may think you're helping by playing *something*, but it can really derail the leader. Good leaders can move beyond the arrangement into totally unplanned places seamlessly, with no train wrecks, when accompanied by a team of sensitive players—it's wonderful! And it's not reserved only for the pros or superexperienced. Again, just by simplifying and listening more to what a leader is doing, you can become a great follower and supporter. Regarding sounds, textures and pads create more freedom and space, plus they come across as tasteful, and *that's what gets you asked back more often!*

4. Keyboard Players. In my case as a leader, I'm not depending on the keyboard/piano to lead or carry a song, because I do that. In this scenario, a more meat-and-potatoes approach is best. Blocked chords and pads provide more color and texture; they embellish! Syncopated or busy rhythmic-oriented parts are cool when well placed, but distracting otherwise. Until you assess what the leader is already providing, "less" is the way to think. One beautiful note sustained can be otherworldly; the wrong sound or

too busy a part can be annoying. The wonderful thing is that there's room for us all to explore and be unique; it's just the time and place that's key. Also the frequency range you normally play within covers a lot of ground already, so a chord creates more fullness, whereas a note adds more texture and definition. On the other hand, if you are in a situation where you carry the band and/or lead from keys, it's a different thing; now you're the glue and have to establish the tone and direction. That means more rhythmic and melodic playing.

5.   Auxiliary players, the often forgotten! For you it's harder and maybe more frustrating, because unless there's room made for you, you often have to make your own. The more seasoned the player, the better that works usually. There are teams, *and I've played with them*, that put just anyone up on stage with no parts written out or road maps of any kind to go by. It's one big party, and parts are left to the discretion, or lack thereof, of each player. It can be anything from wonderful to torturous! Unless you've learned to improvise and have the chops to do it, it's not a bad idea to just keep it simple, pick a few spots to play, and then sit out the rest. Think melody more than riffs and runs. A melody is like a picture, it lasts way longer. It's a good thing to rehearse some spontaneity as well, so when the time comes and there actually is a space, you're more apt to be prepared for it. Since there's not normally as much room created for auxiliary instrumentation, I encourage building in some feature spots around a player's particular ability or some time set aside from the service to explore, and just play. Why should the guitar players have all the solo fun?

6.   Singers. Thankfully, to God, we all sound great! To human ears, we don't all sound good, and sometimes we're just plain bad. I'm not judging hearts here, just musicality.

One of my jobs is session singing. Session singers are brought in to sing background vocals on recordings. A typical session goes like this: we come into a studio with anywhere from one to six singers, listen to a song, arrange or read our parts, then record them. It has forced me to learn to do less and listen way more, which helps me blend better. Everything is more exaggerated and out front in the headphones. You hear yourself *loud and clear*, mistakes and all. It helps that the recording environment is well controlled, unlike some live settings. Singing live requires even more work, not only to sound good, but also to protect your voice and your ears in the process. *Good monitoring is a must to even begin to sound good and well blended.*

Though some leaders intentionally stack a bunch of singers on the melody and have them sing from start to finish, that's not the way I prefer it, mainly for flexibility and dynamics reasons. The more singers, the harder they are to manage, unless you've had the time to rehearse arrangements and parts. Typically, rehearsals for most worship teams barely allow enough time to familiarize yourself with a song, let alone focus time on parts and blending. Honestly, most settings in worship sound like a free-for-all.

I encourage knowing the song sections and building parts as you go, rather than automatically singing on every section. Determine the parts quickly—or ahead of time if possible—and develop the form of the song. By form I mean the road map—for example, verse, chorus, verse, bridge, chorus. Make notes for each section, noting what you're doing, when to lay out, and so on. That way it's easier for the leader to set the pace and for you to complement tastefully and dynamically.

In a choir, the director would prepare and cue you regarding dynamics, but in a team/band setting, it's much less directed that way. Some love the freedom; again, our worship is beautiful to God, and He sees the heart. But we do have a choice of how many notes to use, when to and when not to pipe up, step out, cover up, get in the way, and so on. I'll also say this: when there's a gifted singer who exemplifies taste and discretion, my normal instinct as a leader is to ask him or her to do more! It's just the opposite, though, if a singer is clearly not capable of being sensitive and team oriented.

Let me encourage you as you do whatever you do on the team. Instead of being overly sensitive or insecure about your abilities, be honest and teachable. Until you've had the benefit of time with a leader, think and listen. Until you know what to do, go slow and do less. These are just some things that may help you understand more about what helps and hinders a leader as he or she focuses on hearing God's heart and leading well.

Dial It Down

It's long been said that a good song is a good song. Years back artists began releasing unplugged versions of their songs, bringing back the simplicity long associated with singer-songwriters. It became a genre, and we learned to love some of the new versions as much as the old, because the song still shone through even when wrapped in a different package.

One of my greatest lessons in worship I learned without even knowing it was happening. Being a Church boy, I was always the designated song leader. I only started leading worship after going through my own personal revival along with some friends I met with weekly for years. Together we encountered God in a different and very profound way that would literally change the course of our lives forever. Eighteen years ago, it was standard practice to start our meetings and gathering with music. However, we decided to lay down our instruments for a season to just pray and read the Bible—that's it. One to two years into it, we felt we could pick them back up and play to God as if He were there in the room with us. It was genuine and passionate, and it's really how we learned to worship! We also learned not to lean on talent, sounds, production, performance, and so on. By default we can do a lot of things the way we always have and still miss the real living, breathing presence of God.

By stripping it down to the basics—no sound, lights, or amps—we learned the power of giving room for songs and prayers. It was just us, unplugged. It helped us pay more attention to what we were expressing versus how we were expressing it. In time, a slew of songs came out this raw and organic incubator time with The Lord. They began to spill over into larger gatherings and connected in ways we'd not imagined. They were more powerful than anything we could have ever penned in normal songwriting sessions.

A good thing to do as a worship band every now and then is dial it way down and change up the colors in the palette. I was at a rehearsal recently where we did that out of necessity. It was a small room with no sound system, yet we had vocals, guitars, drums, and amps to deal with. So the drummer used rods, and we all played at a fraction of our normal level and intensity. All of a sudden, we were really listening, and it was very nice. You play differently when you listen and can really hear all that's going on around you. It makes a band better for sure, transforming individuals into a team. Try rehearsing that way sometime.

Though most of our worship programs are *thoroughly programmed*, we can still breathe in new life and offer people more opportunity to engage with God by taking emphasis off the normal and expected. Rather than coming in and switching to autopilot, let's do it differently than we did last week. It's a new day every time we gather. We should anticipate the Holy Spirit moving in and among us as He wills—today.

Another lesson that I gleaned much from was in Eastern Europe at an outdoor festival in 2000. There were hundreds of people from many Eastern Bloc countries, most of whom had lived under the oppression of communism. At one point, it poured down rain, forcing us off the stage and into a circus tent. It was hot, smelly, and buggy—I remember that part well. Totally unplanned and out of the blue, the Greeks started singing a well-known worship song, then it shifted to the Romanians, the Hungarians, the Turks, the Americans, the Dutch, the Polish, the Croats, and so on. It was a volley of worship that transcended instrumentation, production, culture, and language. It became a unifying and defining moment of the event, and it lasted for hours. No one wanted it to end.

As musicians we do play a part in facilitating God's people in worship. Though we can also be a hindrance, I don't think we need to fear using the tools we have to the best of our abilities, unplugged or plugged in! Both the wall of sound and the simplified production are beautiful. We may not have total freedom in our particular worship context, but within the parameters, there is still much we can do to remain sensitive.

Here's a little list of some things to try on for size:

1. Pick a song you know, place it in a different key than you're used to, and let someone other than the normal driver drive it. For example, have the keyboard player lead instead of the guitar player. Everyone else should find a different sound or texture than his or her normal go-to sound. Acoustic guitar: capo up or down and/or play different inversions of the chords you normally use. Electric guitar: try a single-note part or nice melody line. Bass: try using four to five notes only and staying below the fifth fret. Singers: if there are ten of you, build the song so that there are no more than three ever singing at a time. Horns: resist playing all 120 bars of the song; instead, find two to three spots to play a consistent recurring hook/melody line. Drums: use just the kick, hat, and snare for the entire song, and create a simple pattern with little or no subdivision. Percussion: provide the more rhythmic subdivision and color using your toys and cymbals.

    Now, everyone let the song unfold and build—leave some space! Step out of the comfort zones, yet exercise more restraint than ever. It'll be a great exercise.

2. Strip your team down to a few, go unplugged, sit on chairs or in the round with a few mics. Just by your keeping the team small and the volume

down, the congregation will respond differently and feel more a part of the worship expression.

3.   Give the team a day off—they need it, trust me—and have one of your leaders lead very simply from an instrument. It's amazing what happens, especially in large Churches used to big productions, when they're not only invited in but have to carry it more themselves. Things change when the congregation can't disappear as easily amidst the volume and production. Leader: as intimidating and bare as it may feel, linger longer on a section of the song, allowing for prayers and songs to arise.

4.   Memorize the sections of songs, not just an arrangement; rehearse moving from section to section without a form. That means everyone has to listen, to follow and support the others and the leader. The more able you are to deviate from the roadmap without trainwrecking, the better you are as a band.

5.   Try a service once in a blue moon where you ask people from the congregation to start off or suggest a song. Let it go how it goes. Don't plan anything! Giving the people some freedom and responsibility is good and should be more a part of our worship.

Remember, there's no formula for the perfect worship service. Each one of us needs to make it to the foot of the cross daily. The hope is that we can spur one another to encounter God!

Under Pressure

microscopic. So small as to be visible only with a microscope, extremely small, concerned with minute detail.

Most of us are trying hard just to *get free* enough to worship as it is and don't need to feel judged or under the microscope. Yet many of our leaders truly feel under pressure, like they're always being watched. The environment in some Churches is not much different from many corporations. There's an expectation, in the name of excellence usually, to perform the program as scripted without exception or variance. That makes freedom hard to come by, for both leaders and parishioners. We can't parse out all the problems of Church life here, nor do I think I have all the solutions, but to grow with God, we have to start being honest and admit when we have it wrong.

Part of the problem we're up against in the Church stems from building on and perpetuating an autocratic versus Jesus model. Read this definition of *autocratic*: "Of or relating to a ruler who has absolute power; taking no account of other people's wishes or opinions; domineering." Though it may describe someone you know or work with, please resist the urge to run and call him or her an autocrat! You won't make many friends that way for sure.

I'm honored when you share your Church struggles with me. The fact that you're expressing your thoughts and opinions is important—I don't take that lightly. It's my desire to help remind you why we do what we do.

So let's bring it down to the foundation: relationship. Worship is connecting. If we don't connect and commune with God and one another when we gather, then what's the point? For us to connect with God, we have to at the very least feel free to be who we are. If we're trying to be who we are but keep bumping into man-made traditions and styles that don't allow it, we'll only do it for so long before we either blow up or move on. Hence, most Church growth is transfer growth, not new life.

Freedom is hindered when a spirit of control is at the helm of any ship. That management style sends the message that ministry can only be accomplished if *I* do it, if *I'm* in charge. The Church is not a kingdom to be ruled by anyone other than The Lord, who loves, keeps, guards, and leads her with complete and total authority! So the rest of us are what? Just servants, and we either serve or we get in the way. A leader is not a bad or wrong thing; it's God's idea without question. I do, however, question some leaders' understanding of what Godly leadership is. There is a vast difference between leaders that lead with *absolute power and authority, taking no account of other people's wishes or opinions,* and ones who build up and serve. I don't meet many happy people under the autocratic style of leadership, and sadly it has left in its path a wake of former Churchgoers.

With what I do, I get to hear from both the Church leadership—who are annoyed or uncomfortable with too much space in a service—and from the creative leadership, who are bored with the routine and feel stifled and not trusted to lead people anywhere. Pastoral leaders work hard to steward their posts faithfully, meeting the needs of many, not just a few. They do so because they feel responsible as good shepherds do, plus they get the scathing emails complaining about the worship program, worship leader, and so on. Worship leaders work hard to follow the Spirit, facilitate others, and wait on The Lord, which is hard to do if you fear being watched constantly by the powers that be and the people. I can understand the struggle on both sides.

So let's look at what we can effectively change. Each of us bears the responsibility of stewardship. Unity is not agreement on every issue; it's proceeding together in love as one family undivided. If we want the blessing of God, then we have to prioritize and strive for unity as we come to worship. Whatever the chasm or conflict in our particular case, the way forward starts with being focused on getting it right ourselves, not pointing out where everyone else is wrong.

A good leader doesn't have to dictate! Ever been in a band or ministry with a diva or a control freak? Their own insecurities and issues make them blind to healthy relationships, maybe relating in general—so it's only good when they're happy. Dealing with our own unreal expectations, sins, and issues is something we do have control over and can change. As with a marriage, two people bring "stuff" into the union, so the healthier they are from the start, the better chance they stand of sticking together through *certain and impending* conflicts and struggles. God meets and helps the sincerely humble and teachable.

Here are some things I ask teams:

- How much time do you spend together, aside from the musical and technical part of the worship service? I know that not every team has the benefit of time together offstage, but to a large degree, you're only as strong or healthy as your relationships are.

- When's the last time you took the person you have a problem with for coffee? Or genuinely tried to find out what's really happening in his or her life? If you don't know, then what you don't know may have much to do with why he or she does the things that drive you crazy. Mercy always wins!

- How important is for you to be in the team and on the stage? Does it matter a lot when you're not asked, overlooked, or even left out? Sure it matters, but it really shouldn't affect our attitude and desire to engage with God and His people. We should be able to get over it without becoming bitter people or running off in a huff!

- Can you worship in spite of who's leading or on the team or not? Whether it's your style or not? You should be able to, and if you're taking things too personally, it's likely a sign that you have your own problems to deal with.

- Can you lay it down as easily as you pick it up? If you find yourself guarding and protecting your spot or needing it in order to feel good about yourself, you may want to take a season of rest to keep from becoming too attached to your position.

- Good stewardship is honoring our leaders, even if they do stifle, annoy, or bother us at times. We're not responsible for what they do or don't do well. If we've said yes to a position of leadership and are sure God led us there to begin with, then we're there for a reason. Guess what? It comes with the painfully beautiful reality that iron does sharpen iron. It's like any other relationship really. So if we fail our tests, we just may get to take them over another time and season.

The point of worship is not to get through a program without derailing or allowing a lull or silence to occur. God's not impressed with performances—proud of His kids but not impressed. He connects with hearts that are longing and willing to connect with Him honestly. All we do should serve to facilitate the real purpose of gathering; if it doesn't, we need to part with it. Sometimes feeling under pressure is our own deal, but it's also reflective of the need for *air in the Church*—that would be the Spirit of the Living God—so let's make room!

Is It Okay to Love to Play?

Musicians innately love to play; it's a natural, God-given desire. We are exhorted to be good stewards of our talents and excellent in all things; both are very important as leaders in worship. My goal always has been to aim for excellence, be the very best me possible while keeping my heart in check and motives pure. It is okay to enjoy playing in worship, though sadly it's often mistaken by others as performing. But what we're responsible for is the attitude of our own hearts before God, not what others think.

As a professional musician, I am expected to be a team player in the studio and onstage. To be tasteful and mature with my contributions. Listening to and complementing the band, artist, or worship leader. It's important to know what is expected from the leader or artist and not to override their wishes with my "genius" ideas. Since I do want to be hired again, I do my best to have a great attitude. How much more so then in worship should we give the utmost in skill and heart to God and each other. We should prefer and build one another up and not detract from the unified expression as a team. Being creatively inspired is part of God's design, and each team member's uniqueness adds to the offering. Humility and skill together are powerful!

As a worshipper, my goal is to go there myself, honestly and purely. Focusing my heart and attention on God, giving Him glory and thanks for who He is and all He's done. As a worship leader, my goal is to do all of the above *and* help others engage with Him. How and what I play is different in both scenarios. As a leader, I am cognizant that others are following my lead, on the team and in the congregation. I'm still a player, just more focused on leading. I also try to respect and prefer the other players, by making room for their contribution to the team effort. When I'm supporting another leader, I am more focused on helping and facilitating him or her.

The worship stage may be an opportunity to showcase talent for some, though I doubt that's true for most. What human doesn't love adulation and glory to some degree, but the grace of God is big enough to cover that, I believe. It's counterproductive in my opinion to become the worship police, judging others' hearts and motives. Thank God we are free to come into worship as we are and can rely solely on the Spirit of God to convict and deal with us, that's what He does. But it's merciful, never mean! It's impossible for us to bring a perfect sacrifice. For that reason, the writer of Hebrews explains that Christ became the perfect sacrifice, once and for all. So now we have confidence to come boldly into God's presence, as imperfect people.

We can also learn from the Old Testament regarding the excellence of the Levitical priests. The most skilled craftsmen were in fact commissioned for service in the temple and even found themselves before kings. There was great importance placed on the sacrifices and services in the temple and their preparation, because God is holy and worthy of the best. He demanded it, and so required the life of His own Son to be atonement for the sin of all humanity. That's the gospel story truth! So we can't reduce worship down to creative expressions and emotional experiences when it's a life and heart issue. It's still important to prepare practically as well as spiritually, honing our skills and studying to show ourselves approved.

God does allow us to be tested and our weaknesses to be exposed. Usually to those closest to us, because His aim is to perfect our character and transform us into the image of Jesus. That seems to take us by surprise, but it's in the Word, and we should know it. The deep desire we have to play is something we may also have to lay on the altar at some point, and it may be for other reasons than its our identity or idol. We see and know in part down here, so we have to *trust and obey*.

As diverse, unique, and numerous as creatively talented people are, it would be impossible to tout one particular model as the right or only way to do things. Who ultimately knows the secret formula for worship leading and balancing the God-given desire to play? We're all learning and in need of the constant purifying work that comes as we lay ourselves fully surrendered at the foot of the cross. No need to fear our weaknesses, just be aware of and honest about them. We don't aim to please men, but we should pursue excellence in our craft. We also don't trust in our own ability to present the perfect sacrifice of praise; we can't. Jesus promised to lead if we'll follow Him on this journey.

Real balance comes as we grow and mature as believers. It is okay to love to play in worship. I've had some of my best musical experiences alongside other players during worship, in extremely different settings. It's also important to revere and honor the One we do it for; that means weighing our own hearts regularly.

Think Band!

Thinking beyond ourselves is how we become more attuned to the bigger picture. We are not a worship band to simply indulge our own ambition or desire. Rather, we are there to give back to our Creator from our hearts and serve. Though God sees our hearts, it doesn't hurt for our offerings to sound good. No matter the overall skill level of a band, we can do our best, and that's all God is asking.

Things to think about!

- *Think Team:* When possible, I encourage there be enough consistency among a worship band for it to become more than just a cover-band-type gig where everyone shows up and plays the songs. Consistency depends a lot on the organization and commitment of all members. The more a band becomes a team and develops a natural flow together, the more you can follow the leader and go places without being totally tied to a chart. The band will work and play better together if they truly become a team. I suggest there be a point person for coordinating schedules, charts, rehearsals, and so forth. Set some guidelines for all to commit to—you'll know quickly who is committed to the team or just wants to play. Build your team with those who really want to be team players.

- *Think Parts:* Not much sounds worse than everyone playing at the same time, paying no attention to what they're playing in relationship to the whole. It's like painting; if everyone paints the same color, it's a blur. The frequency and timbre of your instrument fits in a certain space on the overall canvas of sound coming from the stage. Choosing the right part is important if you want to be heard and sound good. For example, if a keyboard player uses the left hand a lot when there's a bass player playing the lower register parts already, it gets muddy and loses distinction and definition. Staying on parts above that range causes it to pop out. When there are two guitar players, using capos, alternate tunings, and different voicing helps avoid overlapping. Every voice and instrument occupies a sonic space, which loses distinction quickly when we compete for it.

- *Think Taste:* Songs should ebb and flow, build and breathe. The chart is your road map, and it should be marked with the appropriate signs to help you play tastefully. As the song unfolds, mark sections to play simple parts that support, and then other sections for licks, melodic lines, or more intricate parts. Someone always needs to hold down the fort and be the meat and potatoes of the song. Normally there is one keyboard or guitar player who provides the glue and chord support. Many times it's the leader, but not always. Everyone else clue in to that person, make sure you can hear him or her well in your monitor mix, and let what you do accentuate, not distract. Bass players and drummers: being the foundation, you in essence desert those depending on you to provide stability if you venture out too much. I have one friend who fines his young band members five bucks a fill until they learn when and when not to play; try that on busy players! When playing licks or riffs, be melodic and simple.

The difficult reality for most worship ministries is that we all have lives and are busy people. We can't devote everything to the worship team and shouldn't. So it involves finding the happy medium that works for us. The fact that many teams are comprised of people that may not even know each other or have any kind of relationship adds other dynamics to the mix. Taking this all into consideration, we do what we can to improve and be the best team players we can be. The key is having a desire to do more than the bare minimum to be on the team or only fulfill our individual wants and needs. It falls on everyone to think like a band.

Be Salty

Ever feel like you're losing your saltiness as a player? We are creatures with habits, and sometimes they're hard to break. That includes using the same four chords we learned years ago in every song, playing the same exact riffs and lines, and so on. It also applies to attitude and behavior. We burn out, we feel entitled, we feel deserving; get bitter, jealous, and envious—you name it.

In my estimation, we have developed a whole doctrine around the musical portion of worship and leading. We've become so people conscious that we've removed much of the freedom. It's almost at the point where we need a seminary degree or an appointment from on high to be on some teams. I've written a lot about the heart, and we all know that's where it starts and what God alone sees. What I'd like to address here is more the playing with excellence and skill part of the equation.

The level of musicianship has been improving in the Church over the past 10 years. There are some young talents playing circles around us old guys. I was teaching a seminar for guitar players not long ago. During a break, I heard this 13- or 14-year-old kid playing in the hall and thought about asking him to come teach the class; he was freakishly good. Putting aside competition, which is not what it's about anyway, we can become too comfortable and satisfied with where we are. Maybe even reach the point we stop learning or even trying to be better. I never want to diminish another's efforts or heart to serve in worship. Hopefully you'll read this and feel inspired to do *what you can* to become an even better player and help to your team or band.

Five tips to sharpen your skills:

1. *Improve your chord and scale knowledge.* With good reason, most worship songs are simple and have just a few chords. Still every chord can be played in more than one way or position; inversions are good to study and know for that reason. It's not simply knowing a bunch of chords but knowing how to play the same chord different ways. A chord is made up of a triad: the root, third, and fifth. Inverting just means playing the triad in a different position—for example, third, fifth, root. There are many resources to help you to learn chord inversions; they will help make your parts more interesting for sure. It also helps you voice your chords opposite what other players are doing, which is more like layering than duplicating. Scales help

you develop better dexterity and facilitate melody. Try singing and playing a scale at the same time as an exercise. The more scales you know and can play with ease and freedom, the more it becomes second nature, allowing you to contribute more readily.

2. *Improve your reading skills.* While it's good that most worship songs are easy enough to follow along with just by reading the words with chords above them, many have no idea how to follow a real chord chart. Even if you're not a schooled reader, you can follow a chart if you can count. By chart, I mean a road map of the arrangement as it's supposed to be played, with bars, rhythmic notations, repeats, time signature, and so on. There are books galore with charts of your favorite songs. The difference is, you're following along every bar instead of blindly hoping you place the right chord over the lyric you don't know. Some have good ears and just rely on hearing the song once, then playing by memory. That's fine and may get most players by—again, we're not being legalistic—but it is frustrating when players "hunt and peck" around for what to play. Until they learn the song, it sounds like a mess! Even if they know the song, they likely never play it the same way twice. Especially if you ever hope to work as hired player, reading will always help and improve your chances of being hired.

3. *Learn to construct parts.* Yes, less is more most of the time, but you can still be tasteful and inventive without stepping on an arrangement. I like to think about songs in sections and create parts for each section. It helps to listen first to what everyone else is doing, then find your own voice within the mix. For example, an intro may call for a riff or melody on guitar or a solo instrument, a pad for a keyboard player, and nothing for the bass player. As a band, decide ahead of time where fills and solos go. This will help both incorporate players and avoid their getting in the way of one another's playing. Instead of an "all skate" approach to a song—that's when all guns are blazing from top to bottom—leave spaces and holes. Find your parts for the sections, commit them to memory and/or chart them, then get used to playing them that way every time for a season. Tweaking as you go to fine tune and building from there. I promise that if you come up with one cool line, even a single-note part done tastefully, that's what others will remember most.

4. *Spend time with your gear.* The better you know your instruments and gear, the more prepared you are, and you'll spend less time taking up others' valuable time to tweak. For example, guitar players who use effects: experiment at home with running your time-based effects such as delays, modulation, and reverbs through your effects loop. It's quieter and sounds different from putting them in the chain with your distortion and overdrive pedals. You may find you like it and get better tone. Just Google "Effects Chain." There are bunch of ways to do it, explore them!

   Keyboard players: create five to ten staple sounds, and store them in a performance patch, so you can recall them live at the touch of one button instead of tweaking on the fly.

   Bass players: learn the difference in application between a fretted and fretless bass. They're not necessarily interchangeable for every song. Fretless is a bit like slide for guitar players; not everyone can do it well. Good intonation is imperative, so practice first. Buy a compressor and learn how to use it, it's the main effect you'll see used by most bass players.

   Drummers: I can't say about enough how helpful it is to understand electronics and computers and be able to use them live as adeptly as you use your sticks. It's a matter of using technology to your advantage, which, in many cases, makes you even more useful to the team.

5. *Study up.* For homework, pick two players that do some of what you'd like to do better, study them, find out what you can about their influences, and learn to play what they play till it sounds like them. I'm not suggesting we become copycats, but we can and do learn from others. Ask a better player, someone you have access to, to spend five minutes, thirty minutes, one hour, whatever they can spend, to show you five things they work on or do well.

Finally, sometimes we actually need to take a break from the routine to refresh. It can be a healthy pattern to develop and also makes room for others to grow. Prayer and Google are wonderful tools of the trade too. Add back some salt to your playing, you'll never regret it!

Charts—Worth the Effort

One thing that's proven true for me: I never regret putting time and effort into being prepared. My bad dreams usually involve me showing up for a gig, my amp and guitar are miles away, and I have to carry them up hill—through the snow both ways—before we count off a tune in two minutes. Crazy! But it shows that I hate being caught unprepared for sure.

It's hard to be critical of those who volunteer time every week to be involved in worship at their Churches. Above all else, it's a sacrifice that God sees, and that's what matters. Still there are things we can do better that help the overall excellence factor. If we're doing all we can already, then that's all anyone can ask. Obviously we have lives to live and greater priorities than the worship team. But if we're counting the costs, setting good boundaries, and doing what we commit to do, then there's more we can do. For one thing, we can prepare our music. Worship bands are always revolving, making it hard to have consistency. Charts are normally words with chords above them, which tell you little about the song unless you already know it or play through it a few times. Even if we know a song, every leader's arrangement of it is normally different. As a rule of thumb, I like to know the road map before driving down the road. I can wing it no problem, and sometimes you have to, but it's better to have a heads-up, especially if you're serving different leaders. So I prefer a real chart with bars, repeats, and notation. As leaders, if we expect the band to follow us, we should provide them with either very clear cues or charts with some kind of notation and direction. Or else give them the freedom to wing it and fly by the seat of their pants without letting it bug us.

Music is more interesting with dynamics, and charts help facilitate good dynamics. Even if you're not a reader, you can make notes. At the very least, I do something like this for each song:

Song Title
Key = **E**   **Capo/2**
4/4   120bpm
I   Melody line
1v   Pad / Ethereal
2v   Chunk
C   Eighth notes, delay w/mod
3v   Drivin / Bigger
C   Power chords / Big!
O   Melody line, ends on the 4!

To not know where you are or what you're playing is to be winging it, and that's not a bad thing, but if it affects other players or hinders the overall execution, then just do some homework. More often than not, I actually chart out a song onto one page, using the Nashville Number System that assigns a number for each chord and doesn't require recharting to change keys. Here's how simple a chart can be.

Mighty to Save

Key=G   4/4

I   ‖:   4   1   6-   5   :‖

1v   ‖:   4   1   6-   5   :‖

                4 5   4/6 5/7

C   ‖:   1   5   4 1   6-5   :‖

2v   Same

C   Same

                        ///>>

B   ‖:   4 1   5 6-   4 1   5   :‖   5

C   Same / Down!

C   Big!

Note: underlining a bar means it's a true split bar unless otherwise notated. Meaning each chord gets half of the total count per bar.

Good players can play a chart down having never heard the song and still make it sound good. Not every leader provides good charts. That's why I've learned to write my own. I'm not the best reader out there, but I compensate for my limitations by putting forth the needed effort. *It's not about knowing everything, just knowing what you need to know to do your best.* Over time it becomes second nature and instinctive. In the time it takes to learn to use your cell phone, you can learn the number system. At a glance, here's how it works. (For a more comprehensive look, check out Chas Williams's *The Nashville Number System.*)

1	2	3	4	5	6	7
C	D	E	F	G	A	B

Note: For keys with sharps and flats, we don't normally write out sharp chords; we use the flat of the normal number for each chord in the scale. For example, in the key of D, the normal three chord is F-sharp. If you play an F, it is called the flat three and notated as ♭3 instead of 2♯. The normal seven chord, which is C-sharp, is called the flat seven, and notated as ♭7 instead of 6♯. This diagram will help give you a better picture:

1	♭2	2	♭3	3	4	♭5	5	♭6	6	♭7	7
D	D♯	E	F	F♯	G	G♯	A	A♯	B	C	C♯

Scores are great, but I find that most players can't read them anyway, or they're so long that you need two stands on stage to see them well, who wants that? Most worship songs can be reduced to a one-page chart; however, for songs with a lot of hits, riffs, and other notation, a score is likely best. Most number charts I see actually notate rhythms and accents by placing them above the bars as needed, and that usually suffices. Find what works best for the team you're leading, or teach them how to read.

The way I look at it, even if you're a band doing your own thing, the more work you put into charting out your songs and coming into rehearsals prepared, the more your own ideas become solidified. For leaders, the best thing you can do for your team is take the time to commit your thoughts and needs to paper. It leaves far less to imagination and improvisation, unless that's what you desire.

What makes our worship stand out is heart and passion; what makes it sound better is preparation and skill. There's a lot of room to be creative, expressive, improvisational, and spontaneous. I find that the more prepared I am, the more I can let go, to be flexible to enjoy the presence of God and making the music.

A lot of other people's time is wasted simply because someone doesn't take the time to prepare; try not to let it be you!

Relevant Worship

Being relevant is certainly critical for impacting our world with the gospel. To be relevant, we must be in the world and living loud enough for others see our light. Heaven meets Earth in the person of Jesus; it is His truth that is saving and His presence that transforms. However much we change styles and methods, He remains relevant across space, time, and history.

The Church is state of the art and modern. We know how to worship and have loads of resources available to help us improve skill. In most ways, we are more relevant than ever before in history. There are four areas I want to mention to help us not only maintain relevance, but also remain grounded as we move forward into the future God has planned for us.

1. *Indigenous Worship*

   indigenous. Originating or occurring naturally in a particular place; native.

   God in His infinite wisdom chose not to make all people the same. Creation is vastly different everywhere you go, in every imaginable way, and it pleases Him. Most people groups incorporate dance and music when displaying their culture, uniqueness, and worship. It is part of our humanness to express and create, because it's part of who God the Creator is.

   Many of the songs that become standards in the Church come from movements. Growing naturally from the raw and organic work of God, reflecting through real and ordinary people. They are innate responses of passion and devotion to the Worthy One, often giving voice to those who can't find or don't have their own words. In truth, each of us should be able to find some words of our own to at the very least say "Thank You, Lord, for who You are and all You've done!" Our honesty is certainly more important than our eloquence. I think it's key that we learn to be real with God and for our worship to have its own DNA more than another's. Every congregation has a DNA: a culture, a sound, and a life all its own. Every Church body has its own issues and needs, strengths and weaknesses.

   Those serving God's people are charged first with honoring Him, from the relationship right down to the music. We should strive to attain unity and humility, and somewhere therein to find the voice of our own particular congregation. What we don't want is to become noise to God or be other than who we are.

2. *Simple Worship*

   Technology has given us great tools to use in worship. There's nothing like good sound, lights, smoke, gear, staging, green room, and so on. But tools are not what enable us to reach Heaven. God can hear and see it all with no problem already. All the best stuff can actually steer us off the track if we're not being driven by the right agenda.

It's a normal cycle that we do the same things over and over, until we have worn grooves in the road that sometimes cause us to become stuck in a rut. So I think it's healthy and good to have periodic reality checks; *dial it back to simple!* For example, try losing the big band and multimedia presentation one week or stripping it down and shuffling the deck. It naturally creates an interruption in the predictable service, forces us not to rely on the peripherals of worship as much and to depend more on reaching God's heart by focusing our own first.

Teaching and modeling are important parts of worship leading. Often we're just doing what's expected or conveyed upon us, and I get that, but people need to know from the top down what's ultimately important to us. The more willing we are to simplify and break from the program of worship so as to demonstrate the heart of worship, the more the Church gets it and follows along.

3.   *Pure Worship*

It took me years to begin walking with a better understanding of grace; likewise, it's taken years for me to walk with a better understanding of purity. Though God does work through impure and fallen people, I've learned He's also serious about purity and holiness.

Some of the messiest people I've known are involved with worship leading and ministry, myself included. There've been seasons that I tolerated certain sins in my own life and heart while still on various platforms in ministry. This doesn't mean that God didn't use me, but He did let me bear the consequences of my sins and actions. He has also sidelined me and dealt with me as a good father over the years.

It's not that people can't be messy—we are, we can, and we will be. But we need to take seriously the things we do willfully, over and over again, knowing it's sin yet carrying on as if it won't matter. It does matter and it will catch up to us. In fact it can alter the course of God's best plans for us, as He will let us choose to walk a way other than His, that's the truth. Remember, the Word says: "Do not be deceived, *God is not mocked*; for whatever a man sows, this he will also reap" (Gal. 6:7).

Whether we're cheating, lying, stealing, or overeating—doesn't matter which one—let's be honest about it and confess it. Part of turning away from sin is being sorry for it first, not simply overlooking and ignoring it. Yes, thankfully we come to God the way we are and receive grace, but He's merciful enough not to let us go on in sin unnoticed without effect and correction.

God desires our best and is acquainted with our struggles. He's passionate about our wholeness and sanctification. Lean hard on His mercy, yet also understand: it's not *unmerciful* that He lets us fall hard sometimes in order to expose the things that offend Him. That's His holiness and providence at work; it's also how He protects us.

4. *Indignant Worship*

We are, indeed, part of a priesthood and so should take leading worship seriously. On the other hand, there is no room for pride and arrogance or believing we have it all together. It caused Lucifer's fall, and God hates it, plain and simple. It befalls the biggest and best of leaders and ministries and is something we should guard against vigilantly.

Whenever we experience something great, our human response is usually to tell someone we love about it. We want them to get it just the way got it and share the same excitement. The tendency is to recreate what we had over and over, even in worship. In our zeal, we can truly come to believe that we do know more than others and have something all figured out. Ultimately it separates and hurts others.

The apostle Paul, though he had a lot of reasons to boast, chose only to boast in The Lord and to preach Christ crucified. He didn't spend much time elevating his own ministry or amplifying his supreme abilities.

Worship is not something to own or brand. We can't control it or use it for our own ambitions without confronting the jealousy and discipline of God. Most spiritually abusive leadership comes from having a healthy dose of pride. Let's not become so defensive of a particular style that we hold others in contempt when they don't share our same enthusiasm or belief. The Church must embrace the reality that we are part of The Body of Christ and not one part is complete apart from the others.

Relevant worship is relative to the life we live everyday; if we are transformed by communing with Jesus, then we can be used to bring transformation to others. Let's work hard to keep it real.

Afterword

The truth is, we are blessed to live in the time we do, where the signs of Jesus's imminent return appear more frequently and clearly than ever before. We live this short life not for ourselves but for His pleasure and purpose—it's a blink of an eye, a breath!

Possibility, opportunity, and resource exist in abundance. Affording the privilege to go, do, and be—whatever and whomever we desire. With this gift comes much responsibility. The challenge in life is not to be distracted so much that we lose sight of the time we live in.

Having come from a strongly supportive and Christian home, I understand how valuable family really is. Though not perfect, my family provided a good, safe, and loving environment for me to grow and become who I am. For too many, the word Church doesn't remotely evoke feelings of belonging or family. But Jesus compares the Church to family more than any other institution or example we humanly know and relate to.

The hope is that the Church will grow through our messes to become the beautiful bride for whom Christ will return someday. It really goes beyond hope though; it is a reality already that He sees His family, the bride, as holy and beautiful—messes and all. What that means is that we can't make Him love us more or less than He already does as our father. But we do choose to follow His lead and do as He did. To love how He loves and serve how He served. We choose to live and be as He is—holy!

For the Church to continue shining as a city on a hill and light in the dark, for this and future generations, we need to grow and mature. We don't need more planning and programming but more connecting and belonging. History shows that times change and things happen in our world that inevitably force the Church to return to basics of the gospel of Jesus. We may not be able to do Church or have Church the way we've always known. Circumstances have arisen before that completely altered the landscape and culture of Church around the globe. It may cost us more than we ever imagined in our lifetime. God is always moving though He never changes. His plan to reach every soul with saving truth before He returns is still in effect—it has never lapsed! If we are to be used the way He intends to use us to impact the world during our brief time here, we must be pliable and willing to let go of what isn't working or is hindering us.

It used to be all about the music for me; my whole life has been music, and I still love it intensely and passionately. But the more I live, the more it becomes about seeking the Kingdom of God first, running the race well and seeing people come alive upon encountering the Living God for the first time. Eternity is real and something to look forward to, but in the here and now, we are sojourners passing through a fallen world badly in need of Jesus.

May we live up to the hope and potential that Christ Himself holds for us and do whatever we do in our Church meetings and times of worship for His glory and pleasure—He so deserves it!

—Tom

Play well and bow low, for the glory of God!

—Matt Redman

Index

About Tom Lane and *The Worship Band Book*

"Tom Lane has been at the forefront of the worship movement for the past two decades. In addition to his busy schedule as a worship leader and teacher, Tom has served as my musical director for the past several years, working with bands and training worship teams from many cultures all over the world.

"*The Worship Band Book* is filled with spiritual insights and practical tips born out of Tom's many years of experience on the front lines of worship and church leadership.

"So, whether you're a pastor or part of the worship team, I highly recommend *The Worship Band Book* to you!"

—Don Moen, Worship Leader

"Tom Lane is passionate about God and about offering passionate worship to the Lord. As a multitalented musician and experienced worship leader, Tom knows how to lead groups of all ages and backgrounds to that beautiful intersection our Lord spoke of when He said we should worship God in 'spirit and in truth' (John 4:24)."

—Jim Thomas, Pastor, The Village Chapel, Nashville, TN

"Tom Lane helps me connect with God through his honest longing for God, his excellence as a musician, his beauty as a composer, and his heart of care for people. Add in his depth of experience and gifts as a mentor and there is none better to write a guide for worship leaders and musicians."

—Casey McGinty, Senior Vice President, EMI CMG Publishing

"I have known and worked with Tom Lane for nearly 20 years. Not long after we met, I considered him one of my closest and dearest friends. We have played music together, ministered together, taught together, and shared parts of our lives that only close friends share. Tom is remarkably gifted, a huge lover of people, and someone who knows the value of mentoring others. I confidently and highly recommend *The Worship Band Book*!"

—Rick Cua, Musician; Pastoral Care Pastor, Grace Chapel, Leiper's Fork, TN;
President, Kingdom Bound Ministries, Buffalo, NY

"Tom is the real deal and has been serving the local church for many years. A pastor, musician, worship leader, and teacher with much wisdom and worthwhile advice to share."

—Tim Hughes, Worship Leader, HTB, Worship Central, London, UK

"Tom has served well in so many situations over the years. From small group meetings and local churches to huge music festivals around the world in front of thousands of people, Tom remains consistent in his humble, gracious heart to serve the moment. I'm happy to call him a friend of many years. I've watched him step up and lead worship with authority and grace as well as come alongside and support dozens of artists with excellence and proficiency. *The Worship Band Book* is filled with spiritual and practical wisdom that will help inspire you and your team towards authentic, effective ministry. Tom Lane is a voice you can trust."

—Paul Baloche, Worship Leader

Worship Musician!™ PRESENTS Series

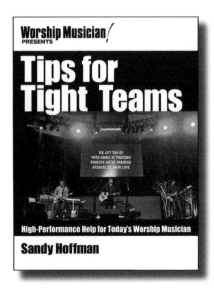

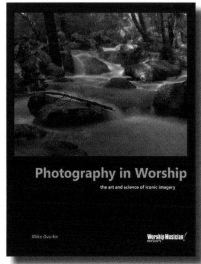

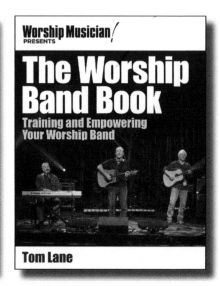

Tips for Tight Teams
High-Performance Help
for Today's Worship Musician
by Sandy Hoffman

Tips for Tight Teams instructs and equips today's worship musician to function on the musical, relational, and technical levels expected of 21st-century worship team leaders and members. Rooted in Sandy Hoffman's "Ten Top Tips for Tight Teams" curriculum, the book covers a myriad of timeless and relevant worship topics. The goal of *Tips for Tight Teams* is to elevate skill levels to the point where the worship team is no longer a distraction to the people it endeavors to lead into worship.

$16.99 • 8-1/2" x 11" • 160 pages • Softcover
978-1-4584-0291-2

Photography in Worship
The Art and Science of Iconic Imagery
by Mike Overlin

The ability to take a photograph – to stop a moment in time – is a very powerful act in and of itself. When this skill is used in the creation of imagery in support of worship, or even as an act of worship, it can be truly breathtaking. This book will teach you the basics of photography through simple explanations and practical examples, and more important, how to "see" the image in advance, with special emphasis on creating imagery for use in worship.

$29.99 • 8-1/2" x 11" • 208 pages • Softcover
978-1-4584-0295-0

The Worship Band Book
Training and Empowering
Your Worship Band
by Tom Lane

Whether you're in a band yourself or part of a ministry involved with teams, this book can help you on your journey. Spiritual, relational, professional, and practical issues relevant for individuals and groups in worship ministry of any kind are addressed head-on. This book will help lay the foundation for a healthier pursuit of creative dreams and a closer walk with God.

$16.99 • 8-1/2" x 11" • 128 pages • Softcover
978-1-4584-1817-3